WEST LOTHIAN

AN ILLUSTRATED ARCHITECTURAL GUIDE

West Lothian is a district of contrasts. The Bathgate Hills separate the rural north, rich in historical associations, from the traditionally more industrial south.

The contrasts are nowhere more evident than in relation to the district's architecture. Linlithgow, Bathgate, Torphichen, the Calders and the small agricultural and industrially based settlements of the district have grown organically over long periods of time. The forces that shaped their form and architecture have been those which shaped Scottish history and industry. In complete contrast is Livingston. Established as a new town in 1962, it is the result of rapid, planned growth tailored to a specific set of social and economic criteria bound up with the need to regenerate the district by bringing in new sunrise industries. The result is a richness and diversity of building and building type, sufficient to feed the interest of modernists, post-modernists or simply those who appreciate fine design of whatever style or period.

This guide covers it all objectively, instructively and at times with insight and humour. The result may be a surprise to those unfamiliar with West Lothian, and a source of pride for those who live and work here.

G I DAVIES
TECHNICAL DIRECTOR
Livingston Development Corporation

© Authors: Richard Jaques, Charles McKean
Series consultant: David Walker
Series editor: Charles McKean
Editorial consultant: Duncan McAra
Cover design: Dorothy Steedman, Almond Design
Index: Oula Jones

The Rutland Press
ISBN 1 873190 25 5
1st published 1994

Cover illustrations
Front: Aerial view of Linlithgow Palace (A & P Macdonald)
Back: Top Houstoun House (Eydmann)
Middle Seagate Micro Electronics (LDC)
Bottom Linlithgow Palace (Jaques)
Typesetting and picture scans by Almond Design, Edinburgh
Printed by Nimmos Colour Printers, Edinburgh

INTRODUCTION

This is one of the finest counties in Scotland. The spirit of agricultural improvement which prevails has contributed in an eminent degree to render it at once the seat of plenty and rural amenity. The anonymous author of this eulogy to what used to be called Linlithgowshire was far from unusual. West Lothian seemed to have a bit of everything to tempt the early 19th-century palate: *its surface has a waving and irregular aspect, and exhibits in every quarter a variety of rich and pleasing scenery* wrote John Leighton in 1831. Pennant, in 1772, had concluded: *The whole is a composition of all that is great and beautiful.*

What, you might think, did they see then that some do not now?

First, they did not speed through the territory in a hermetically sealed tin box, roaring along one of the five parallel east/west routes that have sliced this land like a loaf of bread. To enjoy West Lothian, as did our forefathers, turn aside. Linlithgowshire (now bereft of Bo'ness and Dalmeny) remains very private and can be hauntingly beautiful. Travel from Bathgate to Broxburn, not along the *Great Road* but up over the old road through the hills via Drumcross. You could be in a different world – a world that was once the garden of 17th-century Scotland – dotted with splendid châteaux and manors – Calder, Kipps, Houstoun, Binns, Ochiltree, Midhope and Duntarvie – which clustered around the magical royal shrine of Linlithgow.

Few survive as once they did: and it is upon echoes of a grandeur that you feed at Mid Calder, or in the haunting glen at Camilty. By the plain parish kirks at Livingston or Whitburn, which bespeak the success of the agricultural improvers of the county, or by the secret beauties of Bridge, you can sense an ancient underlying Scotland that has somehow become overlain by new reality.

Our perception is now dominated by that new reality: the leavings of lost industry, visions of industrial dereliction and blackened paraffin-stained ruins. The valley between the Calders and the Bathgate Hills, which funnels into the

Top *17th-century doorway, Midhope Castle.* Above *Pulpit, Torphichen Parish Kirk*

View across the loch to the palace, Linlithgow

T E Gray

The historic skyline of Linlithgow peel: loch, palace, kirk and town house

central industrial belt of Scotland, was the centre of the Scottish oil boom. Generations had known that mineral wealth lay beneath the sparse soil, but in the thirty years after 1850, oil, paraffin, brickworks, coal mines and iron mines erupted like boils: tall chimneystacks, fortress-like chemical works, grim miners' rows, and worthy churches and church halls swamped whatever ancient and desultory settlements once existed. There was money to be made, but – oddly – it does not seem to have been spent in West Lothian. There is little of the immensely grand construction funded by the great industrialists of Glasgow. The money, indeed, appears to have been extracted from West Lothian like the minerals, rather than re-invested there.

These new desultory and unplanned communities were largely workaday; and as the heavy industries have withered, some – whose only possible rationale was profitable local work – have been beached, neglected and forgotten.

Others have regenerated. Amidst all this arises the phoenix of Livingston: a focus of new industry, a new population, and contemporary attitudes to living and landscape. The industrial dereliction has been so totally removed that you get a sensation comparable to looking at somebody who has undergone wholesale plastic surgery: it is not quite natural, but it works and you are left wondering what damage could it possibly have replaced.

The improving aspirations of the District Council to transform its barren wastes into a central Scotland forest, beginning with some of the bings at Addiewell, is entirely in harmony with the improving activities of earlier generations like the mud-spattered tree-planter, Lord Hermand. Who knows, those panegyrics about the beauty, improvement and rural amenity of West Lothian may become as true by 2000 as they were 200 years ago.

There is much to be discovered and enjoyed. The purpose of this guide is to indicate where to look.

The Goth, Armadale

Fooks

Linlithgow c.1812 drawn by
G F Robson

In 1636, Sir William Brereton visited Linlithgow and found it *a fair, ancient town, and well built, some part of it stone*. He admired St Michael *as a fair church* and the palace as *very fair, built castle-wise*.

Organisation of this Guide
This volume begins with Linlithgow Palace, then the High Street (east/west), south and west Linlithgow; north-east to Grange, The Binns and Hopetoun; east to Ecclesmachan and Winchburgh; the Bathgate Hills; the Great Road from Blackridge to Broxburn and Almondell; Fauldhouse to Livingston; West Calder to Hatton House; and finally the Lang Whang running across the rim of the Pentlands.

Text Arrangement
Entries give the name, address, date and architect (if known). Generally, dates given are those of the completion of the building (if known). Lesser buildings are contained within the text. Appropriate demolished buildings and unrealised projects are included. Text in the small column illustrates the history and character of West Lothian.

Map References
References in the index refer to page numbers. The numbers on the maps refer to those against the building entries in the text. Where entries are concentrated, space allows only sufficient numbers for visitors to take general bearings. The maps are intended only as a guideline.

Access to Properties
Many buildings in this book are either open to the public or are clearly visible from public road or footpath. Many, however, are not. Readers are asked to respect occupiers' privacy.

Sponsors
The authors are particularly grateful to West Lothian District Council, Lothian & Edinburgh Enterprise Ltd, William A Cadell Architects, Livingston Development Corporation and the Landmark Trust for their sponsorship of this volume, without which it would have been very much more expensive.

Illustrations
The source of each illustration is noted alongside.

West elevation, Hopetoun House

LINLITHGOW

On a raised mound of almost mystical beauty overlooking a loch, the citadel of palace and kirk still appears the focus of pilgrimage. The burgh's plan is that of a single winding street almost a mile long, swelling at each gate — the East (High and Low Ports) and the West Port — into a welcoming reception point (in the pre motor-car era). Here were the houses, tenements and booths of merchants and tradesmen intermingled with the lodgings of local gentry and clergy, and occasionally those of greater dignitaries requiring to be close to the palace.

Some were arcaded as was customary to Renaissance Scotland. In 1858 David Waldie observed that a Mr Braes *very judicially left open for inspection the mouldings of the arches for what seems to have been an arcade under the upper galleries* on a building near the cross. Theodor Fontane, in the same year, found that the High Street's houses *sometimes painted green and sometimes painted yellow* reminded him forcibly of his German homeland. By then, Linlithgow had lost its pretensions, contracted to a small county town dependent upon craft industry like shoemaking. So the old buildings were thriftily cut down and refronted (or replaced wholesale) by douce classical burgher architecture of little incident and good scale. Burgher self-respect no longer tolerated the *double range of tall, black and grim-looking houses, carrying the imagination back, by their ruinous and antique appearance, to the time*

Above *Linlithgow, c.1680, drawn by Captain John Slezer. The crown remains on St Michael's Kirk, and a timber gallery overlooks the loch and the palace.* Below *The King's Fountain as it may have appeared in the 1530s, reconstructed by J S Richardson.* Bottom *Linlithgow as drawn by Timothy Pont, c.1590. He has compiled several views into one. The western façade of St Michael's and the broad outline of the palace is clearly visible. The huge tower is that of the tolbooth, and the probability is that his sketch of the town was taken from the south and switched back to front*

1

Palace and kirk from the air

Lithgow is a large town, well built, and anciently famous for the noble palace of the Kings of Scotland where King James VI and his Queen kept their court in great magnificence. This court, though decaying with the rest, is yet less decayed because much later repaired than the others ... There is a very great linnen manufacture ... and the water of the loch is esteemed with the best in Scotland for bleaching or whitenening of linnen cloth: so that a great deal of linnen made in other parts of the country is brought either to be bleached or whitened. Lithgow is a pleasant, handsome, well built town; the tolbooth is a good building and not old, kept in good repair and the streets clean. The people look here as if they were busy, and had something to do, whereas in many towns we have passed through, they seemed as if they looked disconsolate for want of employment. The whole green fronting the loch was covered with linnen cloth, it being the bleaching season.
Daniel Defoe, 1723-5

when Linlithgow was a favourite seat of Scottish Kings and when such simple but stately buildings were the town residences of the nobles at court. The contrast between old and new was highlighted by the interspersed modern houses. As the century progressed, so did replacement. Growing romanticism and the cult of Marie Stuart implied that buildings should form an appropriate pilgrimage path to the palace. So, from 1840, Linlithgow was rebuilt in an ever more spikily baronial manner, a romantic skyline the most important aspect.

Linlithgow Palace, mostly 1424-1624
Even stripped of the harl or limewash that once coated its stonework to make it glow like a jewellery box, robbed of its romantic roofscape of ridges, turrets, and tall fleur-de-lis finials, bereft of its statues and stained glass, the gilding of its pediments and dormer heads having rubbed off over the centuries, the palace remains magnificent (colour page C1).

The 16th-century palace, with its large first-floor windows, timber galleries overlooking the loch, and fairy-tale entrance up the Kirkgate, lacked even the token defence of a drawbridge. (It was defensive against very little – hence Cromwell's destructive 1650 *cordon sanitaire*.) It was a pleasure dome on the European model: vivid, pretty, colourful and compact around a courtyard tinkling with its gorgeous fountain.

2

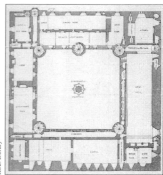

Linlithgow Palace drawn by James Collie, c.1830: Top *The east façade showing the original entrance.* Middle *Elevation of the northern (Jacobean) façade as rebuilt in the early 17th century.* Above *Elevation of the interior of the southern wing with section through the Lion Chamber. Note the alterations made to the façade when Sir James Hamilton of Finnart blasted through the new entrance.* Top right *The plan of the principal floor.* Middle right *North-west corner of the quadrangle showing the King's Fountain, 17th-century northern wing, and Finnart's oddly symmetrical insertions in the western wing.* Right *Internal elevation of the original grand entrance on the east side of the courtyard*

LINLITHGOW PALACE

St Michael's Parish Church and palace from the south. Note the new ceremonial entrance into the palace and the kirk's new steeple

The raised lochside site was certainly fortified by the time Edward I imported James of St George (architect of Harlech) who may have been responsible for the barbican – stumps of whose round towers lie slumped against the eastern façade. In 1424, James I rebuilt the eastern (entrance) wing around a vaulted pend lent symbolic grandeur by great statues beneath cusped canopies. Steps from the courtyard led up to the great hall, or Lion Chamber. Between 1488 and 1513, James IV, perhaps under the guidance of John Frenssh or William Bawty, completed the quadrangle with a chapel on the south and oratory and oriel on the north-west corner.

The palace reached its zenith, 1534-6, under master mason Thomas Frenssh directed by Sir James Hamilton of Finnart. Finnart refitted the Lion Chamber and the chapel: he may have been responsible for the new screen lining the south façade, concealing transes or corridors behind its vaguely Tudor windows, reworking the western wing, and regularising the southern façade. Now that the ornamental finials and statues, stained glass, gilt armorials and painted ceilings for which he was responsible have vanished, his principal legacy is the ceremonial route up the Kirkgate – through an outer ornamented gate with all King James V's chivalric orders, over a paved outer court to another diminutive gateway, through the pend to a new stair to the *piano nobile*, one edge of which is to be seen embedded in the north wall (colour page C3).

The north wing collapsed in 1607, rebuilt 1618-24, by William Wallace in the most fashionable Danish Renaissance; octagonal stair, each window pedimented in gilt, skyline of tall chimneystacks, designed perhaps by Sir James Murray of Kilbaberton. The **fountain**, *c*.1538, comprises an elaborately carved hexagonal well, two off-set stages above, a figure on each angle, decorated by flying buttresses between each stage, culminating in a crown.

You need a lot of imagination and sunny weather to transcend the sometimes damp and dreich – and wholly unnecessary – dereliction of the palace of Linlithgow to appreciate just how fine it was. The imaginative splendours recreated in the royal palace of Kolding in Denmark bring home how wasteful is the historical fossilisation such as we see at Linlithgow. It is no more architecturally or historically valid to leave Linlithgow in the state it is now than to refuse to rebuild St George's Hall at Windsor Castle (colour page C2).

¹ **St Michael's Parish Church**,
principally 1425-1532, probably John Frenssh
Perhaps the finest parish church in Scotland,
first dedicated by David de Burnham, Bishop of
St Andrews, in 1242. John Frenssh, and his
son Thomas, undertook the rebuilding after a
fire in 1424 and work was still continuing to
the chancel and parapet in the 1530s. Cleansed
by the Lords of the Congregation, 1559, it was
equipped with new galleries for town
magistrates, significant merchants, and the
monarch. In 1606 and 1608, it acted as host to
the General Assembly of the Church of
Scotland. In 1638, one of the national
covenants was signed within.

Top *Southern entrance porch to St Michael's showing the oriel to the priest's room.* Above *The ceremonial western doorway split, in the French manner, by a 'trumeau'.* Left *The splendid tracery of St Katherine's Aisle*

LINLITHGOW: St Michael's

Interior of St Michael's Parish Church

It was in Linlithgow that Queen Margaret Tudor with the assistance of Sir David Lindsay, the young Lyon Herald, tried to jolt King James IV into dropping the invasion of England which ended at Flodden. The King *very sad and dolorous* was making his devotion to God in St Katherine's Aisle: *in this meantime, there came a man clad in a blue gown at the kirk door, and belted about him in a roll of linen cloth, a pair of brotikins on his feet, to the great of his legs, with all other hose and clothes conform thereto; but he had nothing on his head, but red yellow hair behind, and on his haffits, which were down to his shoulders; but his forehead was bald and bare. He seemed to be a man of two and fifty years, with a great pikestaff in his hand, and came first forward amongst the lords crying and speiring for the King 'he does need speak with him' ... He leaned down groslins on the desk before him, and said to him in this manner: 'Sir King, my mother has sent me to you desiring you not to pass at this time, where thou art purposed; for, if thou does, thou wilt not bear well in they journey, nor none that passes with thee'. By this time man had spoken the words unto the King's grace, the evensong was near done; and the King paused on the words studying at a given answer. But in the meantime, before the King's eyes and in the presence of all the lords that were about him for the time, the man vanished away and could noways be seen or comprehended but vanished away as he had been a blink of the sun, or a whip of the whirlwind, and could no more be seen.*
Robert Lindsay of Pitscottie, *History of Scotland*

It decayed during the 18th century, making it vulnerable to *restorations* in the 19th. In 1812, James Gillespie Graham demolished the chancel arch, erected galleries in the chancel, a solid wall across the choir, and replaced the medieval timber roof with fake-masonry plaster vaults. In 1821, the superb crown steeple was removed because of threatened collapse. In 1894 and 1896, Honeyman & Keppie sensitively removed the galleries, rebuilt the chancel arch, and added the choir vestry on medieval foundations. Without its crown steeple, the tower looked strangely truncated and, in 1964, Geoffrey Clarke's lightweight, laminated, spiky, timber crown, covered in gold anodised aluminium, was consecrated. The design of the new crown derived *from the skills, techniques and economics of the 1960s. It would form the latest of many additions to the new church, and should be in the same bold spirit as those additions which reflect the time in which they are made. This approach would demonstrate a living church and a living community.*

The church comprises nave, transepts, choir and apse, the tower situated – as in Stirling, Dundee and St Andrews – at the west end, and not over the crossing. Unusually luminous interior lit by its array of triforium and clerestory windows, and glowing with the huge Perpendicular windows of the apse, is broad and spacious. A commanding geometric hand has been at work: like a miniature cathedral,

Opposite: Top *Geoffrey Clarke's 1964 spire.* Middle *New manse.* Bottom *Houses in Kirkgate*

6

the aisles are half the width of the nave and chancel, both nave and chancel are just short of being square. Transept and belltower are both virtually square.

Nave and aisles are continuous, like a vast ship, with a semi-octagonal apse for a prow, entrance tower as poop: the effect enhanced by the way that the beautiful south entrance porch and the two transepts stand proud of the body of the kirk, roofed and gabled, as the aisle roof runs behind. The homogeneity is more apparent than real: look at the elegant south parapet to the choir, probably the work of Thomas Frenssh. The rib-vaulted **south porch** is a gem, niches flanking the entrance, oriel window above lighting the priest's room reached by a circular tower in the re-entrant (colour page C3). The south wall of the **south transept**, or **St Katherine's Aisle** – a plain, square, mystical vaulted space – is almost entirely glass; swirling Scots tracery and stained glass depicting the Pentecost by Crerar McCartney. The effect is absolutely stunning. It is a huge, curved-sided, equilateral triangle containing cusped circles and daggers within, sitting upon six cusped columns. The **west door**, divided by a trumeau (French-style) like Haddington, St Giles and Dundee, is grossly under-appreciated. St Michael the Archangel on the south-west buttress was the only statue to vanquish the Cromwellian dragons.

Twelve consecration crosses elegantly incised in a circle, possibly dating back to 1242, three aumbries (cupboards), a piscina, a window by Burne-Jones, the blocked royal door in the north side leading to the palace, the new screen to the Queen's Aisle by W A Cadell Architects, the ornate Gothic timber pulpit by John Honeyman. In the atmospheric but very regimented **kirkyard**, note the **Livingston Burial Vault**, 1668, with its mort-safe. **St Michael's Manse & Church Hall**, 1974 and 1988, William A Cadell Architects, form a neat group in crisp white harl and grey-slated monopitch roofs.

Kirkgate
Steep processional route between palace and church and the cross. In a **rose garden** is the bronze statue of John Hope, 7th Earl of Hopetoun, and first Governor-General of Australia, 1911, by Sir George Frampton. Early 19th-century classical **Burgh Hall** renovated, along with the Town House, in 1962 by Rowand

LINLITHGOW: Kirkgate

We left Edinburgh with the first train and arrived about 9 o'clock. The morning mists were moving in grey masses through the valley, but they looked like an army in retreat and seemed to be hanging their heads. Sooner or later the sun seemed bound to break through ... The Railway Station lies at the east end of the little town. When getting out, unless you climb to the top of one of the railway cuttings, you will see nothing of the Palace, for that lies on the west side of the town and the view that immediately lies before you is as unremarkable as it can be. A sawmill stands opposite the Railway Station ... The town actually consists of only a single street. Neither the individual houses nor the situation are of the whole in any way remarkable. It is a little town like a thousand others, and if anything in it is calculated to arouse our interest, it is the circumstance that these tenement houses, sometimes painted green, and sometimes painted yellow, remind us of our German homeland and not of the towns of England which, though they have many other advantages, are wearying in their uniformity.
Theodor Fontane, 1858

Linlithgow Cross and Town House. Note the Cross House on the left

Anderson, Kininmonth & Paul. **Nos 1-3** Kirkgate, *c*.1700 or earlier, is an attractive group with painted window and door surrounds.

Cross House, *c*.1700
Town house of Andrew Crawford of Lochcote, framing the ceremonial entrance up to the palace. Three-storey, white-harled and crowstepped, dominated by baroque doorway; geometric plasterwork within. Swelling 18th-century bow-windowed extension to the west, the upper room having a rococo ceiling.

Town House, 1668, John Smith
No other town in Scotland possesses such an imposing civic stage-set. Oliver Cromwell had demolished Linlithgow's old tolbooth with its gigantic campanile in 1650, in an attempt to improve the palace's defences. This splendidly alert successor, one of the most sophisticated burgh buildings in Scotland of its period, is three-storey, with regular pedimented windows, and the six-stage balustraded stair-tower to the rear. **Hardie Hall** within boasts original massive fireplaces with carved overmantels and decorative swags. In 1810, the stone steps were replaced by a delicate iron loggia. After a fire in 1847, much rebuilt by Thomas Brown, the upper spire to the tower being replaced. The 1857 **clock**, by MacKenzie &

Moncur, was the first turret clock in Scotland to be constructed on the same principles as that in Westminster Palace. In 1907, William Scott replaced the iron loggia with the magnificent double staircase. The 1906 **Masonic Halls**, Market Lane, William Scott, has a handsome classical door beneath a masonic emblem.

[Linlithgow] consists principally of one long regular street extending from east to west, gloomy, ill-paved and deserted, though the county town; the antiquity of many of the houses giving it a ruinous and decayed appearance.
J E Bowman, 1826-7

Cross Well: careful 1807 reconstruction of a 1628 original

Lothian Studio

Cross Well, 1807, Robert Gray
Remarkable for the richness and intricacy of the carving, it excites the envy of the citizens of Edinburgh for the copiousness of its supply of water. Gray's design was an accurate replica of its crumbling 1628 predecessor by John Ritchie. Outstandingly flamboyant crown-well sitting upon an octagonal plinth, grouped columns at each corner. Above there is a riot of strapwork, punctuated by amazing squashed stiff-flower finials sitting upon a plinth decorated with animal heads and other carvings. Cusped flying buttresses lead to the second tower in which the corners are marked instead by statues on strapwork plinths: cusped flying buttresses then lead to a domed top decorated with heads, surmounted by the Royal Unicorn. Gray, a one-handed

Anselm Adorne (1424-83) was born in Bruges in the Duchy of Burgundy, of a wealthy Flemish branch of the Genoese crusading family Adorno. Appointed Burgomaster of Bruges, he sheltered the refugee Princess Mary (sister of James III) and her husband Thomas Boyd. When he escorted Mary back to Scotland, Adorne was given life rent of the Barony of Cortachy, further lands in Angus, and was appointed conservator of privileges of the Scots in the Duchy of Burgundy. After his wife died, Adorne pursued his career in Scotland, appointed Captain, Keeper and Governor of Linlithgow Palace and – in 1478 – Lord of Council. He owned land in Kirkgate, Linlithgow, Blackness and Edinburgh but, being embroiled in the struggle between James III and his younger brother, he was killed by dissidents in January 1483 in a priory east of Edinburgh. His body was buried in Linlithgow at St Michael's, and his heart taken to Bruges. His nephew Anselm Sersanders succeeded him as Captain of Linlithgow Palace.
Dorothy Dunnett

Linlithgow is famous for two things quite apart from its Palace – namely its loyalty and its fountains. To whom it has been loyal is rather difficult to determine, but it might well boast of its fountains even today. The most remarkable of these is one, rich in figures, which stands opposite the Town Hall and reminds one of similar work in south Germany. Presumably this is the one that inspired the second line of an old Scottish rhyme:
Glasgow for bells
Lithgow for wells
Falkirk for beans and peas
Peebles for glasses and lees
Theodor Fontane

High & Low Ports, at the east end of the High Street, mark the eastern points of entry to the town – High Port from Edinburgh, Low Port from Linlithgow's port of Blackness. A plaque on the wall of the Star & Garter Hotel relates that the town wall ran between the two gates behind which was the burial ground and the Chapel of the Blessed Mary. Nothing remains above ground.

Linlithgow Academy: Right Original perspective and plan. Below One of the two entrance towers. Bottom Community & Outdoor Education Centre. Bottom right St Michael's RC and Manse

stonemason, had the mallet strapped to his left stump. Adjacent is a contemporary pedestal with a gargoyle with the town's arms and dates, and an inscribed slab by Vincent Butler RSA commemorating the town's 600th anniversary as a royal burgh.

2 **East Port**
Linlithgow Academy, 1900, J G Fairley
Accomplished sandstone primary school in Scots Renaissance: aggrandised cottage with circular, turreted towers *à la* Falkland to signal boys' and girls' porches. **Community & Outdoor Education Centre**, 1987, Wheeler & Sproson, has white roughcast curved walls at the entrance. Large colourful staircase mural within by James Cumming.

St Michael's RC, Blackness Road, 1887, Pugin & Pugin
Gracious grey Gothic revival Puginian box, low set, less bullish and more romantic than those in Stirling and Glasgow; enlarged 1893; modernised, 1952, by J A Coia (who designed the panelled reredos). Scissor-beam roof within.

Regent Centre, 1983, Robert Hurd & Partners
Replaces the Italianate towers and brick arcades of William Scott's 1908 Regent Works for the Nobel Explosives Company, with

10

concrete blocks, mock-battlemented mansard roofs, flying steel arcading and canopied shopping at the rear.

3 **Barons Hill**, 1913, W Scott
In conspicuous position high above Bell's Burn, smart Scots revival in harl and dressed stone – particularly elaborate with lion-rampant panel above the entrance. Lorimer-type roofed round tower and plain dormer windows. Stained-glass, ingle-nook windows, thistle finial, pronounced skewputts.

In 1799, Linlithgow was *ancient, pretty large, regular and tolerably well built. It contains about 2300 inhabitants. Tanning of leather and making of shoes constitutes two principal branches of their employment. Making of stockings, tambouring, and a print field for cotton cloth are also the means of furnishing employment and bread to a number of the people.*
R Heron

Above *John Wood's plan of Linlithgow, 1820.* Left *Linlithgow from the south, c.1680, by Captain John Slezer*

High Port
Ascends the hill under the railway bridge, immediately after which **Back Station Road** doubles back to the split-level station at platform level. The gracious **Linlithgow Station**, *c.*1840, probably John Miller, is a rare first-generation station for the Edinburgh & Glasgow Railway; good stone, cast-iron platform canopy, barrel-vaulted and glazed porch, and south platform waiting-room. Vivid mural by Marie-Louise Coulouris.

The Edinburgh & Glasgow Railway was begun in 1838 and opened in 1842. As normal, it closely followed the line of the canal. Using several deep cuttings, tunnels and two large viaducts, it produced a line that remained almost level between the two cities save for the steep incline at Cowlairs into Glasgow.

Linlithgow Railway Station

4 St Magdalene's Distillery, Edinburgh Road, *c.*1880
Taking its name from the vanished Hospital of St Mary Magdalene, the distillery consisted of two huge, blackened, stone malting-barns (one four-storey, one enclosing a courtyard) and three square kilns capped with pagoda ventilators. Refurbished with adjacent neo-Mackintosh terraced housing, 1990, by Cooper Design Associates.

5 Star & Garter Hotel, 1 High Street, mid-18th century
Substantial coaching inn, three-storey with rusticated quoins, dressed window surrounds and good doorway, picked out in black and white, name hugely emblazoned across the façade. Fanlit entrance. Stabling to the left. Steep climb to the station on the right.

St Magdalene's Distillery: Above *A converted kiln.* Right *The new houses*

9-21 High Street, 1886
Undigested Scots revival block in proper hôtel manner enlivened by an intricate skyline of dormer windows, crowstepped gables and turrets with ball finials atop. Singularly detailed turret at western end – corbelled from a chamfered corner up into square and then up into round; decorative only, apparently no room within. In front, **St Michael's Well**, 1720, the best of the town's wells. The well-head is surmounted by a figure of the Archangel Michael with the town's arms. It is inscribed comfortingly: *1720. Saint Michael is kinde to straingers.*

Below *Star & Garter Hotel.* Right *High Street from the air*

12

The Mint, early 16th century (demolished)
Unusually elaborate town house of the Knights
of St John of Jerusalem consisting of a street
frontage and two courts behind a long and
superbly elaborate hall and the tall tower to
the south-east with an oriel window. The hall
had a splendid open timber roof and an
elaborately carved fireplace.

Post Office, 29-31 High Street, 1903,
W W Robertson
Diminutive Scots Renaissance, too tiny to fill
the space. Handsome doorway and three
splendid dormer windows. Adjacent **33-41**,
good early 19th-century urbanism, plainly
classical with a good doorway to No 41.

47 High Street, 18th century
Large rendered building with quoins, central
pediment and plain, 1815, Doric-pilastered
door. But the margined windows are not quite
right, and imply two separate buildings later
unified behind a common frontage when
translated into a single house with seven
rooms, two bathrooms, a ballroom and a buffet
for Miss Henderson in the late 1850s.

Royal Bank of Scotland, 53-55 High Street,
1859, David Rhind
For Linlithgow, Rhind shed his smart classical
habit for a rare baronial bank, entered through

Top *St Michael on his well.* Middle
The Mint prior to demolition. Left
*Drawing of The Mint interior by
Thomas Ross.* Above *Royal Bank*

Alexander Cornwall is said to have been one of the six knights at the Battle of Flodden who was dressed identically to King James IV, in order to fool the English. The trick worked only too well. Along with his king, Alexander Cornwall was killed.

a tall round, conically roofed tower: principal banking hall, outlined by a stringcourse, has good straight classical windows. Pretty oriel window, square chimneys, dormer windows and diminutive turret at the other side. Unusually wilful for a bank. Rhind was proud of it, leaving his initials DR carved below the angle turret.

57 High Street, 1883
Corbelled, crowstepped tenement on the site of the town house of the Cornwalls of Bonhard recollected only by their family crest, built into the wall at the back of the pend to **No 59**. The inscription reads *Ve big ye se varly*; in other words, *we build, you see, warily.*

20-24 High Street, 1840, is a rather fine row of late-classical houses. Confident ashlar ground floor, a cornice linking all doorheads: one notably bracketed with a geometric fanlight, its neighbour **22** with a splendid round-headed, slightly projecting entrance. Elaborately framed windows above topped by a plain cornice.

36 High Street, late 17th century
Smart town house entered through a round stair-turret at the rear. Harling (picked off) would reveal the inherent geometry of this lovely building: dressed stone frame running up the sides and across the top and acting in counterpoint to the window reveals. Refurbished, 1970, Gordon Duncan Somerville.

6 **Hamilton's Land**, 40-48 High Street, early 16th century
Lodgings of the Hamiltons of Pardovan and Humbie restored by the National Trust for

Hamilton's Land: the town house of the Hamiltons of Pardovan, the Sheriffs Depute to Sir James Hamilton of Finnart in the 1530s: Above *Prior to restoration.* Right *After it*

Scotland, 1958, as part of the *Little Houses Scheme*. Twin crowstepped gables to the street linked by a covered stairway rising between to the principal floor. Projecting window margins of **42-44** reveal it once was harled. The gable of the other has a doocot. **No 46-48** retains a bread oven in the yard behind.

Red Lion Hotel, 50-54 High Street
Pitch of its roof and the size of the first-floor windows indicate a 17th-century building recast in the 19th century when the classical doorway was added. Smaller-windowed extension westwards above pend, with later outsize dormers. In 1820, the lion was a Golden Lion; turned rouge with age and now gone.

82-84 High Street, early 18th century(?)
Steep pantiled roof and heavily modelled windows indicate a very early date for this substantial merchant's house, obscured behind 20th-century drag of PVC windows etc.

Victoria Hall, 1889, J Russell Walker
Built *out of a desire to show loyal regard for Her Majesty in the Jubilee year of her reign*, it cost £2800, and was opened by the Earl of Rosebery. Wildly out of scale with the street of predominantly two- and three-storey town houses, what really mattered was the Germanic skyline of the corbelled turrets and pinnacles sliced off in the 1937 transformation by Alexander Cattenach to the Ritz Cinema, leaving battlements, machicolations, niches, the great window and round-headed door with rope-moulding. Now an amusement arcade.

178 High Street (demolished) showing the outline of the arcades with which Linlithgow, in common with other Scottish Renaissance towns, was once graced

East High Street and Victoria Hall, c.1900

Linlithgowshire Journal, 114 High Street, c.1910
Smart commercial little insertion; a playful parapet with dragon rainwater heads, broken by two large pediments. Ground floor almost entirely glass.

67 High Street, 18th century
In his laboratory above the **Four Marys** bar/
restaurant, the pharmacist Dr David Waldie
conducted experiments with anaesthetics.
Sir James Young Simpson, the pioneer of
anaesthesia, recognised Waldie's chloroform as
being safer and more effective than his own.
The bronze plaque, by R Hope Pinker, 1913,
records David Waldie as *a pioneer in
anaesthetic research – to him belongs the
distinction of having been the first to
recommend and make practicable the use of
chloroform in the alleviation of human
suffering.*

89-91 High Street, *c.*1890,
George Washington Browne
Baronial fantasy of twin gables with
pedimented crowsteps facing the cross, framing
two plain storeys of handsome windows
separated from the ground floor by fretwork.

Above *89-91 High Street. Note the
County Buildings to the right.* Right
*Courthouse and High Street looking
west*

Below *County Buildings.*
Bottom *Plaque to the Regent Moray*

County Buildings, 1935, J Walker Todd
Unspectacularly neoclassical, like an
overscaled town house underscaled for location,
pavilion roof surprisingly undemonstrative in
this street of romantic skylines. Lacks fizz.
Smart interior with good Raeburns.

7 **Courthouse**, 1863, Brown & Wardrop
Prettily romantic Tudor with steep pitched
roofs, spiky chimney stacks, stringcourses and
hood-moulds. Note 1875 bronze plaque, by Sir
Noel Paton, commemorating the assassination
of the Regent Earl of Moray in 1572.

Imperial Cancer Research,
107-109 High Street, 18th century(?)
Substantial harled tenement, dressed stone
margins, ferociously pantiled roof, and two
elegant shops at the base, restored, 1989. If the
gap between the two shops contains an arched

High Street just west of Dog Well Wynd, c.1780, reconstructed by Charles McKean from the engraving by Philippe de la Motte. The gallery of Finnart's town house, on the left, was the building from which the Regent Moray was shot. Left That section of street as it is today

pend, this may be a cut-down and shortened relic of the 16th-century mansion at the corner of Dog Well Wynd.

8 **The Vennel redevelopment**, 1967, Rowand Anderson, Kininmonth & Paul Comprehensive development of 90 houses which replaced 19th-century and earlier houses (1674 stone pediment from the Golden Cross Inn in the wall of the east side of the cross the only memento), in three well-articulated

The Courthouse was built on the site of the town house of Sir James Hamilton of Finnart, c.1496-1540. Eldest (bastard) son of the Earl of Arran, he was head of the Hamilton family from 1529 to 1538, during which time he was a soldier, Lord of Council, Master of Horse, Special Justiciar, Master Sewer and the king's *lovit familiar*. In 1526 he had been made Captain of Linlithgow Palace. In 1531 he acquired his town house which became his seat of operations, and in 1534 he became sheriff. From 1533 his avocation as Scotland's first architect became apparent with his responsibility for major alterations to the palace, the work executed by his master mason, Thomas Frenssh. He was also responsible for castles at Craignethan and Crawfordjohn, and probably at Strathaven, Kilmarnock (Dean Castle), Ochiltree, Greenock and East Kilbride. He was responsible for the stupendous palace for James V at Stirling and used his enormous wealth to pay for it in return for legitimacy. He was executed on 15 August 1540 for treasonably firing a missile, from a machine which he had invented, from the tolbooth campanile in Linlithgow at the king at the front of his host (i.e. army).

Architect's perspective of the Vennel redevelopment, c.1960

The Vennel redevelopment looking east

On 23 Jan. 1570, James Stewart, Earl of Moray, Regent for the baby King James VI (Mary Queen of Scots being exiled in England), was assassinated by James Hamilton of Bothwellhaugh – shot from the house of John Hamilton, Archbishop of St Andrews (Finnart's half-brother). The regent was *en route* back from Dumbarton Castle and was lodging overnight in Linlithgow. The Hamiltons, principal supporters of exiled Queen Mary, regarded the Regent as the prime obstacle to her reinstatement, and Bothwellhaugh had a personal grudge because he had been dispossessed by the Regent's soldiers and his wife ill-treated. He planned to use the timber gallery overlooking the street. The Regent attempted to turn up Dog Well Wynd to take the back road to Edinburgh but found it blocked: and by the time his horse reached the house, the press of people was so great that it was moving very slowly indeed. He was shot through the belly and died just before midnight. Bothwellhaugh escaped to Hamilton, and then went overseas. The house (almost certainly Finnart's own house) was partially burnt by an enraged mob, but still existed almost 250 years later.

groups with shops, library and health clinic, concealed parking areas and garages, offering intriguing views through to the shimmering waters of the loch. Its open character destroyed the enclosure of the High Street, and shattered the drama on emerging from an enclosed funnel into the swelling cross. Yet the harled courtyards, more appropriate to Linlithgow than most post-war redevelopment elsewhere, were extraordinarily ambitious in trying to recapture the quality of a major burgh rather than the large shoemaking village it had become. The High Street frontage needs to be sealed again if it is to recover its sense of place. Saltire Housing Award, 1969.

From the **Water Yett** eastwards, much plain classical of the old-fashioned variety, mostly stone, but some colour-washed and some with good round-headed dormers. Some, like **No 218**, are early 19th-century burghers' houses.

Oliphant's, 216 High Street, 19th century Attractive shopfront for one of the last of the Linlithgow baxters (or bakers) of which the town once had 16. **212**, with its fanlight, Doric doorway and broad coach pend acts as a handsome introduction to this long sedate row of good, plain classical houses. To the rear of 212 is the remains of a contemporary **tannery**, only survivor of the 17 Linlithgow had in the 18th century. Good views to the rear of the varying length of the Long Rigs may be had from the lochside.

Baird Hall, 1863, Brown & Wardrop
Baronial schoolhouse tamed as a house with
two gabled dormer-headed windows.

123-125 High Street, 18th century
The oak-leaf emblem of the cordiners, inset
into No 123, recalls how Linlithgow was second
only to Perth for tanning and shoemaking.
Shoemakers' Land, No 125, a handsome,
substantial early 18th-century mansion,
restored, 1975, by Gordon Duncan Somerville
would be further enhanced by restoration of its
original limewashing.

**Bo'ness for blethers, aye and
Linlithgow for leathers**. In 1772,
Thomas Pennant noted the town's
*considerable trade in the dressing of
white leathers*. Leathermaking may
have been brought to the town by
Oliver Cromwell's soldiers in 1650,
and the use of the oak leaf insignia
recollected its use in the tanning
process. After tanning, Linlithgow
cobblers, known as *snabs*, made up
the shoes. Nor was it just single
orders. In 1773, the Earl of Hopetoun
ordered 700 pairs of boots for the men
of his regiment. Nor just shoes either:
long before Lochgelly, Linlithgow was
the tawse-making capital of Scotland
– its three, five- and seven tailed
instruments concentrating the
thought of local youths. Remains of
one of Linlithgow's two tanneries lie
behind the High Street, beside houses
and the loch. In one of the pends can
be seen hooks for unloading the
heavy hides, and the metal runners
for dragging them down to the works.

Linlithgow Loch
A very special and popular place in
itself, the hour walk around its 100
acres of shimmering water a hugely
enjoyable and invigorating experience
affording ever-changing views of
palace, town and hills beyond as well
as glimpses of the flora and fauna,
duck particularly, in which the loch
abounds. One of the few remaining
undrained natural lochs in the
Lothians. Designated a site of special
scientific interest.

*Left Shoemakers' Land. Below St
Peter's Episcopal*

9 **St Peter's Episcopal**, High Street, 1928,
Dick Peddie & J Walker Todd
Unexpected visitation from the Orient (built as
St Mildred's), Byzantine in massing and Celtic
in detail. Set back from the street, tightly
squeezed by its neighbours, and peeping
timidly down the vennel opposite to the Loch,
its heavily carved and columned door is
surmounted by a huge thermal window, capped
by a buttressed, towered rotunda.

Annet House, 143 High Street,
late 18th century
Local history museum in a plain classical
house with fanlit and pilastered door. Granny's
attic within (and twice as fascinating). Render
cloured off. Long rig walls to rear retain early
relics.

T D Anderson, 163 High Street, John Duncan Victorian butcher shop with excellent pictorial tiling of local scenes.

Right *Decorative tilework of Linlithgow in the butcher's shop, 165 High Street*. Above *19/21 Lion Well Wynd*

10 **Lion Well Wynd**, opened 1750
The best of the town's remaining uphill wynds, built to afford southern access into the town for the itinerant trader. All houses are 19th-century, tight, steep and picturesque. Particularly pretty are **Nos 15**, **16**, **17** & **19**, restored by William A Cadell Architects for the Grange Conservation Company. The curved wall at the top of the wynd faces the buttress of the railway embankment as **Union Road** peeks across the top, and answers its flanking, curved-cornered cottages.

Union Road
Car-squeezingly narrow, wedged between the long back rigs of the High Street, and the embankment wall of the railway, bounded to the north by what remains of Linlithgow's Town Wall, some of its 17th-century doorways entombed within. Principally small houses and cottages; blue-painted **No 5** has pretty porch and dormers with octagonal chimneypots. The confluence of stone walls where Union Road hits the head of Lion Well Wynd is a townscape treat.

Below *5-17 New Well Wynd.*
Bottom *St John's Church*

11 **New Well Wynd**, noted for its 18th-century ashlar wellhead with a pyramid top, is lined on the west by well-grouped, well-scaled 1950s stepped, terraced houses by Rowand Anderson, Kininmonth & Paul. The top of the wynd is marked by **St John's Evangelical Church**, 1840, Romanesque in detail upon a classical plan, the roof corbelled in a manner identical to the single bay in Victoria Place; and **Lindisfarne** (entered from the Wynd), *c.*1845, an opulent classical United Presbyterian manse with Doric-columned porch, string-

course and thin pilaster strips. The tidy **263
High Street**, with its late 18th-century plaque
in the wall, has finely scaled windows and
swept dormers. Restored by William A Cadell
Architects, who also restored **5-17** New Well
Wynd.

West Port, 1968, Rowand Anderson,
Kininmonth & Paul
Masses well up to the corner of **St Ninian's
Road** and the West Port, successful principally
by reason of the geometry, the carefully
contrived stone base-courses, plinths, sensitive
landscaping, tree planting and timber
spandrels to the windows.

West Port and West Port House,
c.1920

12 **West Port House**, 1600
L-plan, three-storey town house of James
Hamilton of Silvertonhill. If the date is correct,
gun-loops etc are anachronistic. Its geometry is
diminished by being robbed of its coat of harl.
Plainly elegant, like a miniature Houston
House with swept dormers and crowsteps on a
steeply sloping roof, it is enlivened by a
corbelled rectangular stair rising from the first
floor in the angle to the rear. Once the road in
front was lowered in the 18th century, the
house gained an added elevation, towering over
its diminutive neighbour to the east, **293 High
Street**. Restored and owned by Thom Pollock,
it is an early 18th-century stone cottage with
crowsteps and pantile roof.

LINLITHGOW: South
Until the early 19th century, Linlithgow was
bounded on the south by a steep hill up which
short wynds clambered, then stopped
breathless. The canal and then the railway
provided a demarcation line beyond which the
town's lawyers and burghers could build their
pleasant and occasionally palatial villas. The

*A confrontation of masonry: the
meeting of Union Road and Lion
Well Wynd*

A G Ingram

Jaques

Top *Canal Basin and the refurbished Canal Terrace.* Above *Hugh Baird's house*

The Edinburgh & Glasgow Union Canal was begun, after much controversy, in March 1818, to provide Edinburgh with cheaper building materials and coal by joining it to the Forth & Clyde Canal near Falkirk. Its engineer was Hugh Baird, salary fixed at £500 per annum provided the canal was finished within five years at a maximum cost of £240,500. He completed it to time, the cost increased by having to dig a tunnel in Falkirk to avoid the Callendar Estate, and by the three great aqueducts over the Avon, the Almond and the Water of Leith, which were designed by Baird with advice from Thomas Telford. The canal was 31½ miles long from Port Hopetoun in Edinburgh to Falkirk, all at a single contour save for the (vanished) locks at Camelon, west of Falkirk. Its economy was killed by the Edinburgh & Glasgow Railway, which opened in February 1842, and sliced harshly between canal and town. The canal was finally closed in August 1965 with the intention that most of its bridges could be replaced by culverts. The section between Linlithgow and Winchburgh was re-opened for recreation in May 1973.

higher they rose, the more spectacular the view – Linlithgow almost invisible in the foreground as Airngarth Hill and, in the distance, the snow-capped Ochils convey an appearance of alpine grandeur in winter.

13 Canal Basin
Surely one of the most pleasant places in which to linger in this lovely burgh – tranquil canal atmosphere and splendid views to the palace – bounded on the east by Bridge 43, to the south by the **Canal Museum** (*c.*1820 stables for the canal horses) and to the west by **Canal House**, *c.*1835, a standard three-bay villa (home of Hugh Baird, the canal engineer) distinguished by its round-arched door and splendidly sinuous fanlight. To the north the basin is bounded by **Canal Cottages**, *c.*1840 (built as the Union Canal Inn), which are split-level, one floor entered from the towpath, and the other from **Canal Terrace** (rather like the Colonies in Edinburgh). Restored by Gordon Duncan Somerville, *c.*1974 (colour page C4).

14 Ross Doocot, Learmonth Gardens, 16th century
Built by the Barons Ross of Halkhead, probably on the tail rig of their lodging. A circular beehive doocot, its thick rubble walls contain 370 nesting boxes, bound by three projecting rat-courses, rather like stringcourses. Recent lantern on top. Gardens commemorate Alexander Learmonth, Provost of Linlithgow, 1802-7. **Wellbank**, *c.*1850, is a pleasant cottage framed by two sets of three square chimneys, and a pedimented skewputt.

Gowan Cottage, Strawberry Bank, *c.*1835 Delightful stone cottage in beautiful ashlar, framed by impressive triple chimneystacks on the octagonal. **Peer Gynt**, 5a Strawberry Bank, c.1890, one of two semi-detached villas balanced around a central pend. Bay windows at each end enriched with startling *in situ* concrete crudely designed to look like timber boarding (perhaps the first deliberate board-marked concrete in the country – later fashionable in London's South Bank).

1 Royal Terrace, c.1865
Pretty single-storey stone cottage, with bay windows and bargeboarded dormer windows, fine bracketed porch. Adjacent **Nos 3 & 4** are grander villas with simple fanlights. To **No 5**, possibly Matthew Steele added a three-storey Arts & Crafts bookend. Pavilion roof with ball finial, solid harled columns on either side, virtually glazed between with beetle-browed overhanging eaves. But for the tile-hanging, and the traditional window-fenestration, the concept is worthy of Mackintosh. Real quality if restored to brilliant white harl.

Top *Detail of the extraordinary board marking in Peer Gynt.* Above *5 Royal Terrace with its Arts & Crafts extension.* Left *6 Royal Terrace*

¹⁵ **6 Royal Terrace**, 1829, John Lauder
Charming classical villa reminiscent of the centrepiece of a new farm steading. Polished ashlar, gigantic semicircular over-arch within which the fanlit front door is recessed, sidelights like a Venetian window. Oculus above, capped by a diminutive pediment. Elegant interior, fine hall with winding stairs.

7 Royal Terrace, c.1860
Two-storey villa with projecting bay and Doric balustraded porch, heavily quoined bay to the east surmounting an arched pend to coachhouse and service court behind.
8-11 Royal Terrace (originally Bellevue Terrace) are well-mannered late-classical with

Canal facts
Labourers on the canal were nicknamed *navvies* – i.e. those who worked on the navigations – and Burke and Hare were amongst their number. The **canal** is approximately 5ft deep and 14ft wide with **walls** formed of tamped clay 20in thick. Its **water** comes from **Cobbinshaw Reservoir**, six miles west of Mid Calder. **Winding holes**, or large inlets, are provided at regular intervals as turning points for barges. With **stone mile posts** giving the distances from Edinburgh and Falkirk, the **journey time** from Edinburgh to Glasgow in the express fly-boat took just under thirteen hours, at a cost of 7½d.

Top *Roseland Cottage.* Above *Victoria Place.* Right *Douglas Cottage, originally the Cottage School*

Friarsbrae, one of the loveliest parts of Linlithgow redolent of the leafy tranquillity and nostalgia that clings to this part of the canal, was originally called Cadgers Road (the customary route of itinerant pedlars or cadgers). Its current name derives from the Carmelite Friary of 1401 that once stood in the grounds of Nether Parkley. It climbs steeply from the junction of Royal Terrace and Strawberry Bank, doing a switchback over the canal at bridge 44, and offers excellent views along the canal in both directions. Interesting bits and pieces of canalside cottage, some stone, some colour-washed, particularly to the east.

stern porches. The retention in **No 10** of the original window-glazing bars demonstrates the importance of these proportions. **13**, originally **The Bield**, is a Gothic cottage – i.e. pantiled with pointed windows. Its large neighbour, **Roseland Cottage**, *c.*1820, is whinstone with freestone dressings with Gothic-glazing window patterns within the classical frame.

Victoria Place, *c.*1840
Beautifully scaled lane to Rosemount Park (lovely views to the palace) leads behind some delightful villas; the first an idiosyncratic, three-bay, two-storey house in beautifully polished ashlar, curious window and door surrounds, geometric fanlight and lying 16 (horizontal) paned glass. **Douglas Cottage**, built as the Cottage School, is an enchanting Tudor pavilion overlooking the canal. Hood-moulded and stone mullioned windows. Proud octagonal chimneystacks.

Handsome stone villas at **1 & 2 Friarsbrae**. **Craigmailen, No 3**, a neat semi-detached villa, has elegant ironwork above its single-storey bay windows. **Svenskbo, No 4**, *c.*1936, fashionable 1930s bungalow with elaborate round-arched entrance and smart round-cornered drawing-room bay.

Poldrait, Preston Road, 1889
Bay-windowed, L-plan villa with Scots revival details. Good interior plasterwork and stair balustrade.

Preston House, 1844,
David Bryce & William Burn
An elaborate asymmetrical composition in Bryce's earlier Burn-influenced style. Mainly two-storey, with prominent crowstep gables on

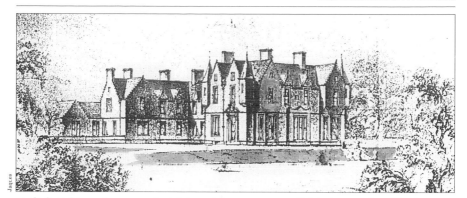

Original perspective of Preston House

each façade, each corner heightened by a square or circular turret. The entrance is huge and Renaissance: and the chamfered bay windows are corbelled out to the square above. The ground floor of the west façade is almost entirely glazed with a swelling bow or conservatory. Stone screen on each side of an archway with a bellcote, festooned with ivy and surmounted by exceptional strapwork, conceals the kitchen from the house.

Thistle glue was once produced at the Gowan Stank Works that stood behind the slaughterhouse in Preston Road. The glue had a reputation for such strength that it was used by the Royal Company of Archers, the Queen's Bodyguard in Scotland, in the manufacture of its bows.

[17] **Rivaldsgreen**, *c*.1840
Vaguely Elizabethan in the early manner of William Burn – skyline of octagonal chimneystacks, a cross finial to the gable, and tall dormer window-heads – large, L-plan, stone villa set at the end of a long drive, pleasantly scaled courtyard to the east. A two-storey hipped bay faces north over the gardens, as does the handsome entrance porch in the angle. First-floor windows are pedimented, and the lofty chimneystacks are angled and grouped.

The Rivaldsgreen Tan Works (long since demolished) occupied a site to the west, by Barkhill Road and Royal Terrace. Barkhill derived its name from tree bark used in the tanning process, which was stacked there.

Clarendon House, Manse Road, *c*.1820, with additions
Retirement home at the end of a beautiful drive through wooded grounds. Inchoate mansion with double-columned Doric portico and entablature, flanked by later single-storey balustraded bays. In *c*.1875, an Italianate three-storey tower was added to the west. Good interior. Two-storey modern extension with conservatory to the east. Smart **lodge** with hood-moulded windows.

Rivaldsgreen House

Rockville Grove, 1982
Intelligently grouped houses in a mature setting with good quality brick, oversailing timber-clad first floors and brown tiled roof. **Rockville Lodge**, in the stone estate-wall, has

a good bracketed porch to the pavement. **Alderley**, *c.*1810, is pleasant, plain classical. **Friarbank**, possibly built in its grounds, *c.*1840, is smarter late-classical with pavilion roof, lying paned glass, pilastered and fanlit door, and fashionable gate-piers.

18 **Nether Parkley**, 1881, Wardrop & Reid
Bourgeois villa burgeoning with details – quoins, oriels, pilasters, pediment and a fanlight. Extensive service wing re-uses an ogee window-head, putatively from the Carmelite Friary whose site was in its grounds. Pretty bargeboarded **lodge**.

LINLITHGOW: West
West Port
Level triangular space, once principal reception area into Linlithgow from the west. The **Black**

Bitch and the **West Port Hotel** are 18th-century relics gazing gloomily upon a spot whose spatial qualities are destroyed by roads, railings and traffic. The black-and-white Black Bitch consists of two two-storey houses, one with swept pantiles, the other heightened in the 19th century with mansard roof and dormer. The West Port Hotel occupies a row of cottages with six bargeboarded dormers and mock stonework.

Top *Nether Parkley. In the foreground lie the faint outlines of the excavations of the foundations of the Carmelite Friary.* Above *St Ninian's, Craigmailen.* Right *West Port*

The Craigmailen congregation, technically the Second United Secession Congregation, was established in 1738, and originally worshipped in the open air at a place near Witches Craig, about three miles south of Linlithgow, now marked by the Craigmailen stone. They came in from the cold, first in 1742, and rebuilt their church in 1805. In 1845 they united their congregation with St Ninian's: and in 1874 constructed their fine new kirk.

19 **St Ninian's Craigmailen**, Falkirk Road, 1874
Simple essay in First Pointed Gothic with wide nave, and attractive tower with broach spire. South aisle and semi-octagonal hall added in 1901. Some good stained glass by James Ballantine, 1885, at the east end, in tribute to Thomas Chalmers, the paper-maker who inhabited nearby **Longcroft House**.

20 **303-325 High Street**, 1-3 Preston Road, 1937, W M Scott
Strong Scots revival council houses marking the junction with Preston Road: two three-storey rubble blocks with dormer windows frame the

corner by cut-away crowstepped cat-slide roofs which slope dramatically from a gabled four storeys to one storey at street level. A stone wall links the blocks at the corner. Plaque depicting the Black Bitch adorns the west corner.

Ashley Hall, Bathgate Road, *c.*1908, William Scott
Janus-faced Edwardian villa of undigested quality: half-timbered bay and adjacent balconied gable overlook a walled garden with an almost Mackintosh-like oriel high in the gable. Entrance firmly Scots – the door flanked by a crowstepped gable containing a giant shallow-curved stair-window. Converted, 1986, by William A Cadell Architects.

Braehead Estate, early 1950s, comprises the neat Swedish semi-detached timber villas favoured by the SSHA since the 1930s, with their cat-slide dormers and smart, white-painted porches containing little seats. The elegance of the window surrounds shows just how little is needed by way of careful design to create something which blends with rather than destroys the environment.

Mains Maltings, Mains Road
Characterful stone and slated buildings; pagoda ventilators surmounting a steep pavilion roof incorporated in housing development. The 19th-century **Mains House**, opposite, a good plain stone villa with dressed window surrounds and columned porch.

303/325 High Street, corner of Preston Road

The Black Bitch is the official crest of Linlithgow. In 1673, the Lyon King of Arms confirmed that the burgh's emblazonment consisted, on the one side, of the archangel Michael, with wings expanded treading on the belly of a serpent, the head of which he is piercing with a spear in his left hand with the motto *May the might of Michael establish us in the heavens*; whereas on the rear of the burgh's seal *Insculped in a field of gold, a greyhound bitch sable, chained to an oak tree within one loch proper.* Those born in the burgh are still proud to refer to themselves as black bitches.

Katie Wearie's Tree commemorates a cattle drover (or perhaps just a girl who followed the drovers) who, coming into Linlithgow market, would wash her feet in the cattle trough, and then enjoy a rest under a leafy green tree just outside the West Port. Saplings from that tree are cultivated to this day.

Left Ashley Hall. Below Timber-built Braehead houses. Bottom Mains Maltings

Falkirk Road contains several villas, some Victorian mansions and more besides. Baronial **Viewfield**, 1888, has a crisply cut monogram and elegantly fretted bargeboarding above. **Highfield House**, finely honed Tudor with a red tiled roof lies opposite. White-rendered **Rodsdale** has a black margin to the deeply recessed basket-arched porch.

Above Rodsdale. Right Longcroft House

Below Jock's Hill. Middle 16 Jock's Hill Crescent. Bottom Public Hall

Longcroft House, Falkirk Road, *c*.1850, David Bryce
A house of two personalities: confident three-storey Italianate tower to the west, attached to a sprawling hunting lodge with baronial details.

21 **Jock's Hill**, Jock's Hill Crescent, 1932
Red rosemary-tiling and dominated by a corbelled brick chimney. Asymmetry of a later extension has given the house an Arts & Crafts appearance. **16 Jock's Hill Crescent**, 1988, J McFadyen, is a swaggeringly Swiss, brick and deep-red tiled villa with three tiers of dark-stained timber balconies clustered around its central chimneystack. Huge steeply sloping roof ties all together into the wooded hillside.

22 **Chalmers Buildings**, 2-14 Main Street, 1907, Sir Robert Lorimer
Good example of Lorimer's cottage style, for papermill workers, in white harl and swept slate roofs. Prow-shaped dormers are slate-clad and hung – with the usual diamond motif. Gables hipped and eyebrow-eaved. The **Public Hall** (community centre), across the road, is also by Lorimer in 1907: a harled rectangle, the sides consist of four huge windows with ogee-roofs rising into the roof, punctuated by battered buttresses. The gable to the street has a lunette window rising above the entrance porch.

Chalmers Buildings

Linlithgow Bridge

The village of Linlithgow Bridge grew after the establishment, in 1786, of a calico-printing works, which soon employed 200 workmen. But its fortunes fluctuated, and scant trace survives. The **bridge**, completed in 1960, replaced one of 1660, built by Alexander, Earl of Linlithgow. Overshadowing all is the magnificent **railway viaduct**, 1841, by John Miller, which strides across the Avon Valley, its 23 arches, some up to 90ft high, overshadowing the remains of the Manuel Nunnery.

The Battle of Cannachy Bridge (often mis-called the Battle of Linlithgow Bridge) was fought on 3 Sept. 1526. The Earl of Lennox, with associated nobles and supporters, was attempting to rescue King James V (reputedly with his encouragement) from the control of the Chancellor of Scotland, the Earl of Angus. Angus, abandoned by the other nobility, hatched a hasty alliance with his feudal enemy, the Earl of Arran, on the promise of much power and spoil to the Hamilton clan, of which Arran was head. Lennox's army was wrong-footed in having to cross the haugh of the Avon and the steep slope on the other side, where his troops were met by Arran's, probably led by Sir James Hamilton of Finnart (Lennox's cousin). Lennox's troops were swiftly defeated and, after surrendering, Lennox himself was killed, probably by Finnart possibly as the result of a heated exchange in which Finnart and the Hamiltons were accused of betraying the King for their own personal gain. Gain there was. Finnart was awarded the Captaincy of Linlithgow, and the extensive lands of the Lairds of Houston and Keir which were among those forfeited.

Left Burghmill House & railway viaduct. Below *Bridge Inn*

Bridge Inn, late 18th century
Substantial inn in white render and black window surrounds, with external stair, one of the traditional stages of the annual Riding of the Marches on the circuitous way via Linlithgow Cross to Blackness. **Manuel Haugh farm** presents three white-washed gables to the road, the house being at the rear of the courtyard.

23 **West View**, 1968, Lawrence Alexander
Six flat-roofed courtyard houses in brick and

black-stained timber. **Burghmill House** is plain and substantial; would be much improved by the restoration of its harling.

West View

Avonmill House
Splendid Gothic cottage with dormer windows and good window bays, somewhat overwhelmed by its later neighbour. Standing marooned by the entrance to Bo'ness Road is a tall yellow-stone 1913 block of shops and flats.

Glenavon House, Falkirk Road, c.1880, ?J G Fairley
Large mansion paternally poised above its mill in the valley below, framed by good stone walls and solid oak Gothic gates. Long and slender it appears to have been L-plan extended into T-plan. Vaguely Scots square bartizan, hood-moulds and chamfered corners, completely overshadowed by the principal entrance with its bargeboarded porch, magnificent glass, etched stonework and great glazed windows into the hall behind. Renaissance dormer window, scrolled chimneystacks and ogee-roofed two-storey bay overlooking the valley.

Glenavon House

LINLITHGOW: North-East

24 **Bonnytoun House**, *c.*1840, ?David Rhind
Gay villa blending mercantilism with
romanticism on ancient site facing across to
Linlithgow Palace. Flamboyant porch fusing
17th-century Renaissance with classical,
leading into a house whose square plan is
entirely concealed by its picturesque skyline –
gables, finialed dormer windows and splendid
octagonal chimneystacks. Cool late-classical
interior with splendid staircase. **Bonnytoun
Farm**, possibly contemporary, a seemingly
single-storey *ferme ornée*, has all the
characteristics of a late-Regency dower house.
Bonnytoun Cottages, 1907, a row of four
single-storey improved farm-workers' cottages,
symmetrical, like Kingscavil, Arts & Crafts
with sweeping roofs and small-paned windows.

Left *Bonnytoun House.* Top *Interior.*
Above *Bonnytoun Farm*

25 **Sun Microsystems Ltd**, Blackness Road,
1990, The Parr Partnership (colour page C6)
Less of the lightweight pavilion floating in its
incomparable site than it might have been:
hard-edged subdued blockwork, metal cladding
and glass computer-assembly factory and
offices sunk into the site to minimise impact.
Civilised and light interior with magical views.
Extended, The Holmes Partnership.

26 **Grange**, 1904-9, J N Scott &
A Lorne Campbell
A magnificent expression of confidence, Grange
bestrides Airngarth Hill, displaying an
accomplished re-use of the 17th-century Scots
Renaissance details of the second Scots revival.
Designed for Henry Moubray Cadell, it is a
lovely place; harled with stone dressings, and
all the necessary ingredients – open pediments,
crowsteps, datestones, crest and balusters.
Lavishly furnished interior – plaster ceilings,

William Cadell (1708-77) was one
of Scotland's earliest industrialists,
founding the Carron Iron Works in
1759 jointly with Dr John Roebuck
and Samuel Garbett. The lease and
subsequent purchase of **Grange
Estate** in 1778, principally for its
ironstone, allowed the family to
pursue activities already
undertaken in East Lothian.
Nineteenth-century heirs of this
distinguished family include the
geologist Henry Cadell, author of
The Rocks of West Lothian.

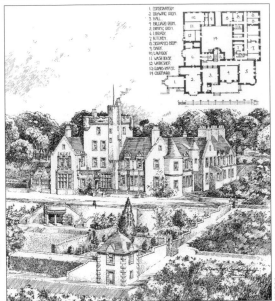

Right *Original perspective of the Grange.* Top *Hope Monument.* Above *Earl o' Moray Hotel*

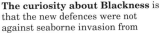

marble chimneypieces, splendid wood panelling. Conservatory, parterre, rhododendrons, architects' office and terraced ornamental gardens sunk into the hillside. The **Hope Monument**, Airngarth Hill, 1859, conspicuous three-stage octagonal Gothic space-shuttle with wolf gargoyles, commemorating Brigadier Adrian Hope, killed in India, 1858.

Earl o' Moray Hotel, early 19th century
Extended from a thick-set late-classical white-rendered villa with piended roof and chunky pilastered porch. Pleasant Regency-detailed stair within. Originally **Bonsyde House**, it was once the home of the explorer Wyville Thomson.

Bonhard, 1591 (demolished)
Diminutive L-plan château – seat of the Cornwalls of Bonhard – formerly just over the slope from Grange; had large apartments with graceful 17th-century plasterwork on the principal (first) floor.

27 **Champany**
Created from a pretty, possibly 17th-century single-storey pantiled steading. Whitewashed courtyards, and restaurant within the refurbished octagonal horse mill. Between here and The Binns, several small L-plan

The curiosity about Blackness is that the new defences were not against seaborne invasion from England or France, but against landward attack by Scots. Utterly different in character from the defenceless palaces erected elsewhere for James V, it underscores the intended role for Blackness as the principal state prison beyond Edinburgh Castle and, perhaps, intended to replace it. This was to be Scotland's Tower, its Château d'If, its Alcatraz. It was also particularly well placed, by a port, to deliver its undesirables into exile.

bungalows, *c.*1930 – no doubt Ministry of
Agriculture smallholdings for First World War
soldiers.

[28] **Mannerston**, from 16th century
The external appearance of an Improvement
farm with baronial flavouring. Do not be
deceived. Mannerston was a place of substance,
at least by the early 16th century when Sir
James Hamilton of Finnart was its owner,
whose remains were probably rescued and
translated into what looks like a farmhouse,
with a pilastered doorway. Fine 17th-century
plaster ceiling by the same craftsman who
worked at The Binns.

Mannerston

[20] **BLACKNESS**
Former port of Linlithgow, most of whose
buildings post-date 1800. The square has an
Arts & Crafts restaurant, the standard *good
inn, c.*1810, and 1876 cast-iron baluster pump
and lion's head drinking fountain. **Nosirrom
Terrace**, is a block of distinctly art nouveau
tenement flats for workers possibly implying
the hand of Matthew Steele. **Blackness
Mission Church**, 1901, J P Goodsir, was built
for sailors; plain, grey-harled with octagonal
steeple. **Blackness House**, *c.*1830, is a pretty,
classical pavilion-roofed villa with unusual
single-storeyed, curved bay windows.

*State prison of Blackness: Below The
heavily fortified landward approach.
Bottom The castle and all that
remains of the ancient port*

Blackness Castle, from 15th century
A sea-provisioned and sea-protected state
prison, whose plan is in the extraordinary form
of a ship, originally on a virtual basaltic island
and entered through a wide (now blocked) gate
in the east flank; *c.*1449, a four-storey almost
square tower was added at the centre, which

Right *Blackness Castle from within: an inhabited courtyard with well and cottages.* Above *As it is today*

In the early 16th century, the Captain of Blackness was Sir Patrick Hamilton of Kingscavil, bastard brother of the Earl of Arran. The dashing adversary of Sir Anthony D'Arcy de la Bastie in the chivalric jousting at Stirling Castle in 1507, he became Keeper of the Rolls, and chief counsellor to his half-brother. He was slain on 29 April 1520 in Edinburgh's High Street, when escorting his half-brother (acting Regent on behalf of the Duke of Albany, who was in France) to open Parliament. Opposed by the Douglases who feared outlawry by the Parliament, fierce fighting – known as *Cleanse the Causeway* – ensued, in which 70 people were slain. Arran and his son, Sir James Hamilton of Finnart, were chased from the capital on a collier's pony. Kingscavil's son, Patrick, Abbot of Fearne, became Scotland's first reformist martyr, burnt in St Andrews in 1528.

Stories of Tam Dalyell's *trooking with the Devil* are legion, and the policies of The Binns are populated by myths and spirits. His boots have a tendency to walk if removed from home. But he was also a man of taste, education and refinement, who experimented with gardening and arboriculture; and enjoyed four unusual marriages. Legends of the *killing times* have tended to distort our perception of him.

may always have been intended as the prison cells they were to become. In *c.*1535 major works by Sir James Hamilton of Finnart fortified it against landward attack: a new vaulted entrance carefully guarded by a spur, corbelled turret and protected emplacement; thickening of the south wall for artillery defence with casemates; substantial governor's lodging above. Elegant staircase and western wing added *c.*1542, leading up to the fine door into the large, well-lit governor's chamber, with its aumbry, and adjacent chapel (later kitchen) behind, its ogival Gothic piscina. Crowstepped barracks now provide shop (colour page C5). *Open to the public; guidebook available*

30 **House of The Binns**, from 1612, ?Sir James Murray of Kilbaberton
Lovely U-plan Renaissance villa created by Thomas Dalyell extending eastwards from a small, probably L-plan tower. It remains the seat of the Dalyells. A king's favourite, constructing a villa near the king's palace at Linlithgow, he may well have used the king's architect, Murray of Kilbaberton. Half a century later, General Sir Tam Dalyell further extended the building. All was clothed in fashionable castellations in 1812 by Robert Burn. Possibly entered from the north, one of the turnpike stairs on that façade was originally corbelled from the first floor. The principal block, harled with stone dressings, was two-and-a-half storeys above ground-floor kitchens and cellars which can still be seen on the west.

General Sir Tam was responsible, probably, for the creation of living rooms in place of cellars, which were later transformed into the Laigh Hall and the adjacent business room (raising the ceiling and thereby squashing the

Left *The Binns from the north-east.*
Above *From the south*

principal floor). The glory of the *piano nobile* is
the two great Renaissance chambers with
outstanding plasterwork by Alexander White –
particularly the deep, elaborate frieze in the
High Hall, the King's Chamber and the
Vaulted Chamber. Painted panelling and
ceilings. The first country house to be donated
to the National Trust for Scotland (colour page
C6). *NTS: open to the public; guidebook
available.* The 1829 **Binns Tower**, in the
same livery as the house, was built by Sir
James Dalyell, 5th Baronet, following an after-
dinner wager. **Merrylees Cottages**, a
characterful row enlivened by obelisk capped
skews, hood-moulded windows and door at the
centre.

Philpstoun

Old Philpstoun retains much of its charm – a
cluster of stone and pantiled dwellings at the
very edge of a wood, and **East Philpstoun
Farm**, a white-rendered, window-margined
Improvement farmhouse. Only a gable
remains of **Philpstoun Mill**, 1784. The
village of Philpstoun grew with shale mines
and oil works at White Quarries. Brick
cottages of mine and railway workers spread
out on either side of the wooded dip of the
Pardovan Burn. **Castlepark House**,
centrepiece to the village on its fine burnt-girt
tump, is an opulent bay-windowed Victorian
villa with baronial touches possibly
incorporating an earlier house.

The flowing locks of iron-clad
General (Black) Sir Tam Dalyell
(1615-85), *bluidy Dalyell* to his
enemies, dominate the Dining Room
(colour page C6). Despite objections
to Charles I's forced introduction of
the Book of Common Prayer into
Scotland, he took the King's side
and was imprisoned in the Tower of
London after the Battle of
Worcester. Escaping, he went abroad
in 1654 and took an oath never to
cut his hair or beard again until a
king was on the throne. He spent 12
years in Russia, during which he
reorganised the Russian army and
was promoted to General. A noble of
Russia, he was summoned back to
Scotland in 1666 to defeat the
Covenanters at Rullion Green,
commended by Charles II *for the
happy success you have had against
the rebels in Scotland*. He resigned
when those to whom he had given
quarter were shot. In 1679, he
became Commander-in-Chief of the
Forces in Scotland and in 1681
formed the Royal Regiment of Scots
Dragoons, better known as the
Royal Scots Greys, which had its
first muster at The Binns.

Philpstoun

35

Pardovan House, 1879
Sober Victorian villa set amongst the chestnut trees: relics of 16th-century Pardovan built into the steading.

31 **Philpstoun House**, 1676
Utterly charming white-harled U-plan house, slightly dumpy because its original vaulted ground floor has been filled in. Probably built for John Dundas of Philpstoun (initials over the former entrance), it feels as though it lost some of its pizzazz in the 18th century. Sundials at each of the three angles. Lectern doocot.

32 **Craigton**, 17th century
Once smart, harled, L-plan, crowstepped villa, Victorian porch and inserted ground-floor windows. Staircase in the re-entrant much cut down, like the dormer windows. Fine rhododendron walk and sundial. Tree-lined avenue leads to ornamental gate-piers.

Top Pardovan House as sketched by Timothy Pont. Above Philpstoun House. Right Duntarvie in the 19th century. Note the splendid balustraded viewing platforms

33 **Duntarvie**, early 17th century
Ruins of a typically long Scots Renaissance lodging (a rare straight stair leads from the front door to the principal floor) flanked by two wings symmetrically placed against the north façade, each with a balustraded flat top and turreted turnpike stair corbelled from the first floor. Unusually handsome **farmhouse**, c.1855, with crowstepped dormer windows and porch.

34 **Abercorn School & Schoolhouse**, c.1860
Unusually pretty, lightly spiky, Gothic school, like a miniature monastery.

Below Craigton. Right Abercorn School

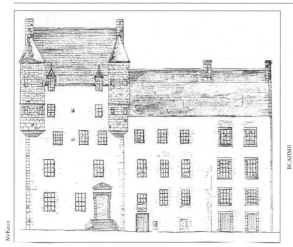

Midhope: Left *An elevation as it might have appeared, c. 1670, reconstructed.* Above *View from the outer gateway*

35 **Midhope Castle**, from 16th century
Midhope's long, rectangular, tenement-like appearance dates from the 1678 re-casting and extension of the 16th-century château. John Hope removed a southern entrance tower, raised the eastern wing with its pre Binns-like plasterwork, extended it with two bays of regular-margined windows, a pilastered corner and panelled chimneystacks, added a new entrance doorway, with its splendid cartouche, a new internal stair and a fine new courtyard entrance. The turrets, as in Ochiltree, are ashlar gazebos – here two storeys high. Consolidation by William A Cadell Architects.

ABERCORN
A hallowed spot, secluded in bosky privacy, Abercorn slumbers as a homely hamlet of Hopetoun. Here was a 7th-century monastery, seat of a bishopric 681-5 (for 200 years as a foundation belonging to Lindisfarne Priory.) The kirk may occupy the site. A Grahame **castle** arose on the far bank of the Hope Burn but leaves no trace. A tiny estate village, on the ancient coast road from Queensferry to Linlithgow, of cottages, houses, high walls, higher trees and – dominating everything – a substantial L-plan Scots revival **factor's house**, c.1855 (colour page C7).

36 **Abercorn Kirk**, from 11th century
As Norman parish kirks go in Scotland, Abercorn must have been a fairly substantial example – wide nave and choir, the latter tenanted by the splendid **Hopetoun Loft**. Most of what you see is by Peter MacGregor

Below *Abercorn Kirk and village from the air.* Bottom *Interior and Hopetoun Loft*

Hopetoun aisle

Chalmers, 1893. Two stained-glass windows by Douglas Strachan, 1921. Fine 12th-century **south door**, chevron stonework in tympanum, and **west door**, 1893, in ferociously crisp Norman with grimacing gargoyles. Aisles sprout from the torso so much as to conceal it; the **Binns aisle**, 1618; the **Philpstoun burial enclosure**, 1723; the **Duddingston aisle**, 1603; and the **Hopetoun aisle**, 1707. The Hopetoun Loft occupies the chancel and faces down the kirk displaying the magnificence of its panelling and fretwork screen by Alexander Eizatt, and the armorial achievement painted by Richard Waitt. The adjacent aisle is a two-storey, harled piece of swagger by Sir William Bruce, complete with pyramid roof, ashlar-panelled windows, and a wonderfully panelled retiring room above burial enclosure below. Atmospheric arboreal kirkyard.

Above *Sir William Bruce's design for the east façade of Hopetoun House.* Below *East front of Hopetoun House*

37 **Hopetoun House**, begun 1699-1701, Sir William Bruce
A truly princely mansion whose urn-capped balustrading, like a shimmering mirage, gradually rises from the landscape as you approach. As you reach the ha-ha and guardian sphinxes, carefully contrived to inculcate a sense of majesty, it reveals itself in its full splendour. Entrance front is predominantly William Adam, and sons John and Robert.

Bruce's façade was shorn of its pedimented, arcaded portico, pavilion roof and cupola, and was refaced with a dramatic skyline of urns and balustrades that caused people to refer to Hopetoun as the *Scottish Versailles*. William Adam's enormous new screen-wall with its huge, unbalustraded flight of steps, its round-headed windows and giant Corinthian pilasters succeeded in transforming a country seat into a palace. John and Robert replaced Bruce's convex flanking wing and offices with much larger concave colonnades terminating in new **pavilions** which, with their pedimented centres, flat roofs and slightly old-fashioned cupolas, pay homage to Bruce's original façade.

Sphinx-eye view of the approach

The handsomest (house) *I saw in Great Britain; the front is enriched with pilasters, the wings of some distance joined to it by a beautiful colonnade, one being the stables, the other the library. The great improvements round the route are very extensive; but the gardens are still in the old taste: trees and shrubs succeed here greatly; among others, two Portugal laurels 30ft high. Nothing can equal the grandeur of the approach to the house, or the prospect from it.*
Thomas Pennant, *A Tour in Scotland,* 1769

The west front, with its axial views and its pond, is largely as Bruce designed it. Three flanks of Bruce's Hopetoun stand proud, the façade with a central round-headed pediment flanked by diminutive pediments on each flank, with a dumpy and very continental effect. Roofscape and chimneys may not be original. The excellent quality of the stonework is attributable to Tobias Bauchop (colour page C8).

Bruce's interior is best in the outstanding octagonal timber-panelled staircase-hall, probably the assured work of Alexander Eizatt, the top landing of which is flamboyantly exuberant with scrolls, pediments, pilasters and mouldings reproducing, in timber, Scottish Renaissance motifs we are more accustomed to seeing in stone. Modern *trompe-l'oeil* panel paintings by William McLaren, 1970. Magnificent painted baroque ceiling rediscovered by Rab Snowden from overpainting. Plainly elegant and well-proportioned rooms with timber-panelled interiors under simple coved ceilings; particularly the lovely garden room and dining room. The Adams recast the principal entrance hall and created what are now the Great Bed Chamber and the Yellow and Red Drawing Rooms – both by Robert after his return from Italy in 1758.

Extensive, beautiful **policies**, best viewed from the rooftop above the north pavilion (originally stables). Ornamental west garden between the house and the Round Pond. To the north lie the north deer park, the bog wood, the bastion walk and the wilderness; to the east the lime avenue, and to the south, another deer park. **Main gates**, 1893, by Robert Rowand Anderson, flanking quadrants with Tuscan columns and crowning vases, and an

Below *Bruce's original stair.* Middle *Main Lodge.* Bottom *Main gates*

impressive over-panel incorporating the family crest. The **main lodge**, also by Anderson, is a doll's house with pedimented porch. The **lodges** – west, east and mid – are in ashlar, with slate roofs projecting over angled bay windows and grouped octagonal chimneystacks. The **service courtyard** has a fine long steading, 1774, with lofts over arched shed openings, a pedimented slaughterhouse (now squash court) and a workshop, 1740. **Walled garden** basks peacefully as a garden centre terraced down the slope to the burn (excellent café). Here you can buy life-size marbly nudes should your fancy extend.

38 **Staneyhill**, *c*.1630
Fragmentary relic of the outstanding seat of the Shairps of Staneyhill; octagonal stair-tower with buckle-quoins, strapwork, superb broken pedimented doorway of a highly fashionable house, possibly by Sir James Murray of Kilbaberton or William Ayton. The **Obelisk Gates** may well be Staneyhill's.

The **mausoleum**, 1829, by William Burn, a heavily shouldered, Gothic, vaulted and stone-roofed monument guarded by crouching and snarling griffins; the adjacent **Temple of Peace** a delicate wrought-iron dome supported on a ring of Corinthian columns. **Butlaw Lodge**, a pretty *cottage ornée*, projecting round entrance with classical porch, round-headed windows and conical (perhaps originally thatched) roof, has a striking Scots extension to the rear, 1972, by Michael Shepley, much influenced by Peter Womersley's doctors' surgery in Kelso.

Top *Staneyhill*. Middle *Staneyhill door: note the buckle-quoins (harling restored)*. Above *Butlaw Lodge*. Below *Hopetoun thatched lodge*. Right *Society*

39 **Society**, 18th century
White-harled, L-plan house (or inn) on the old road from Queensferry to Linlithgow; circular tower in the angle and improbably conical roof, overscaled dormer window-heads and finely cut

stone dressings, *c.*1840. Something older in the western block, and possibly much older in the east wing. **Easter Society** is an utterly charming spot on the waterfront amid chestnut trees at the edge of the Hopetoun estate. APRS award-winning conversion of three stone cottages by Graham Law into a most elegant house (colour page C7).

40 **Digital**, 1988, James Parr & Partners
Computer fortress gazing over the Forth to clones at Rosyth. Embedded in the green rolling slope running from Newton to the shore, amidst luxurious pools and soft landscaping. Crisply detailed with white, horizontal, concrete panels.

41 **Duddingston House**, *c.*1810, Robert Burn
In the most mock of picturesque Gothic, its narrow verticality implies a recasting of the earlier seat of the Dundases (1655 dormer-head embedded in the south wall), confirmed by the fact that the first floor is taller than the ground; customary during the Renaissance. This crenellated shoebox is likely, therefore, to represent a fashionable retrofit. Symmetrical **steading**, 1822, with comparable military insignia. **Ice house**, 1825.

NEWTON
Estate village, probably relocated here following late 18th-century enclosures; with white-harled *good inn*, picturesque cottages, some bargeboarding – a rustic arcadia, crucified by heavy traffic. 1880s cottages for miners of the Whitequarries shale mine.

Woodend
Terraced cottages, mullioned and decorative bargeboarded porches. Kirk (demolished): **Norwood**, 1885, manse by H J Blanc.

Top *Easter Society cottages.* Middle *Digital.* Above *Duddingston House.* Below *Woodend Kirk and cottages*

RCAHMS

LINLITHGOW: East
Gateside Farm Steading

Improvement farmhouse, with a later gabled porch to its fanlit doorway. Elegant whinstone **steading**, much still as originally built, with cart shed, covered cattle courts and granary.

42 **Kingscavil Cottages**, Edinburgh Road, 1873, J C Walker

Enchanting terrace of long low cottages with a delicate chapel-like schoolhouse at the far end. Grouped under sweeping roofs as a single composition, punctuated by dormer windows and chimneystacks.

Top and above Kingscavil cottages & school. Right Champfleurie. Below Champfleurie stable block. Middle Scheme for Champfleurie by Robert Adam. Bottom Hiltly

43 **Champfleurie**, 1851, ?David Rhind

Charming house with an air of much greater antiquity (ancient Kingscavil may be incorporated). An L-shaped russet-hued *jeu*

Soane Museum/RCAHMS

d'esprit, entered through an ogee-capped round tower in the corner. Plain and graceful decoration (remarkably similar to Bonnytoun House – see p.31) restricted to the entrance. Chimneystacks and the finials on each gable. Tudor **home farm**, 1845, pantomime crenellations, hood-moulds and chimneystacks.

Hiltly, late 17th century

Dignified 17th-century house (lacking harl and dormers) enfolded by an 18th-century steading, circular stair-tower to the rear. Elegantly classical gate-piers. Restored, 1980, G McNeil.

44 **Ochiltree**, from 16th century

Once-handsome Renaissance château, extended, truncated, its turrets spliced to the roof and shorn of its harl. As in Midhope, its ashlar turrets or gazebos should have been set off against harling. The proportion of its main chamber is 1:2 – a proportion of which Sir

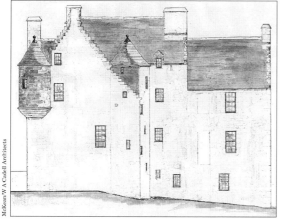

James Hamilton of Finnart was particularly fond (he had these lands 1526-40 following the forfeiture of Stirling of Keir). Two great chambers above each other, above a kitchen and cellar floor; and probably entered by the round staircase in the corner. In the 17th century, the château was enhanced by a courtyard, decorative dormer windows, a new internal stair and an outstanding (if heavy) ashlar porch, surmounted by two finialled pediments, monogrammed SAS and DGS for Sir Archibald Stirling of Keir and his wife Dame Grizel Stirling, probably 1610.

Bridgend Farm, early 19th century
Graceful Improvement farm, pavilion roof and thumping chimneystacks, pilastered porch, fanlit door, single-storey wings symmetrically disposed. Baronial **steading**, rubble, slated, with overscaled, crowstepped dormer windows.

Ochiltree: Left Eastern elevation as it might have been: restored by Charles McKean. Top The porch, limewash reinstated. Middle Interior. Above From the air showing the formal garden

45 **Oatridge Agricultural College**, 1972, Colin Webster
Cascading down its green slope like a new university with the concrete geometric shapes, slender mullions, monopitched roof, bays and clerestories inspired by ACP's Students' Union in Durham. The search for richness in later development has not been accompanied by

Oatridge Agricultural College

comparable control. **Forth**, a court in white concrete blocks, is a self-conscious, contemporary farm steading; arcaded entrance wing, outsize crowstepped pavilions, and a hexagonal seminar room projecting like a horsemill.

[46] **Binny House**, *c.*1840, perhaps Richard Crichton

Now a Sue Ryder home, this seat of the Stewarts of Binny, built in creamy Binny stone, has all the trappings of a Regency villa (pavilion roof and great tall chimneystacks) given a later front; a Doric porch flanked by projecting, balustraded two-storey bays. Curious extensions to the east with oculi, blind arcading and round-headed dormer windows. Flanked by two blind-arcaded pavilions, the **stables** are dominated by a semicircular pediment on brackets, trimmed with oversized diabolo-shaped urns (colour page C7).
Mausoleum, 1873, is a plain Gothic façade to a burial chamber set in the rock of the hill (colour page C8).

Binny House

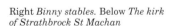

Opposite *Scotland's Château d'If, or state fortress. Blackness Castle photographed from the sea (Historic Scotland)*

Right *Binny stables.* Below *The kirk of Strathbrock St Machan*

Ecclesmachan

Ancient settlement nestling by its burn in a fold of the hills, Ecclesmachan's name may derive from the Celtic *Eglwys St Machan*. Of the kirk **Strathbrock St Machan**, dedicated by Bishop David de Burnham in 1244, only two blocked doorways on the south façade outlined by chevron mouldings, and the elegant rectangularity survive. Venetian window set in blocked Norman arch (to chancel?) on east gable. West chancel added, 1908, by Honeyman, Keppie & Mackintosh. Predominantly 1822 and 1908 in character. Some fine stained glass, 1905, A Ballantine, and 1954 & 1964 by William Wilson. **Manse**, 1850s, is gracious, harled, L-plan house with stone margins, corner pilasters and

Jaques

Historic Scotland

Above *Linlithgow Palace from the east by Richard Jaques.* Left *Sir James Hamilton of Finnart's 1535 ceremonial entrance to the palace*

Above *A Renaissance skyline:*
Linlithgow Palace and kirk.
Right *Palace kirkyard and fountain,*
showing the old eastern entry

C2

Top *Oriel of the priest's room, St Michael's Parish Church.* Above *Inside the royal apartments re-fashioned in 1535.* Right *A slice through historic Scotland: Torphichen Preceptory at the bottom, the spires of Linlithgow at the top*

Top *Western Linlithgow and the Bathgate Hills.*
Above *Linlithgow canal basin by Richard Jaques.*
Left *16th-century oak ceiling, from a demolished
High Street house, Linlithgow*

Top *Sun Microsystems Ltd at night.*
Above *General Sir Tam Dalyell, the*
'bluidy Muscovite'. Right *State*
apartment in The Binns, with its
early 17th-century plasterwork

Jaques

Jacques

Stuart Eydmann

Graham Law

Top *The hamlet of Abercorn by Richard Jaques.* Middle left *Cauldhame Farm.* Above *Stable block at Binny House.* Left *Easter Society*

Stuart Eydmann

Jaques

Thom Pollock

Top *Sir William Bruce's façade of Hopetoun House from the Round Pond.* Left *Binny Craig by Richard Jaques.* Above *Niddry Castle*

chimneystacks: altered by Brown & Wardrop, 1858, who added the graceful ashlar pedimented porch. Parts clearly predate 1800. Note the rolled skewputts. It was the birthplace of Robert Lister, 1794-1847, the celebrated surgeon, whose father was minister of the parish.

Smiddy Cottage, opposite the kirk, a long pantiled range, large rubble stones exposed, converted by Walter Wood. **Schoolhouse**, 1840, hints of enlargement by Keppie & Mackintosh in the pyramid roof rising up into a lantern and a swelling dormer window jammed up against a tapered chimney.

Twelve Mile Lodge, c.1800, looks like a single building: yet it seems to have been two (two front doors) joined by a pavilion roof and fine pedimented porch on three Doric columns.

Glendevon Farm, 1820, James Anderson Estate farm for the Earl of Hopetoun, set amongst trees south of its own secret lochan alive with ducks and swans. Dignified like a villa with classical door and fanlight, it lacks the grandeur originally proposed.

Top *Ecclesmachan Schoolhouse.* Middle *Smiddy Cottage.* Above *Glendevon Farm: original drawing.* Left *Waterstone Farm*

WINCHBURGH

Before the arrival of the shale industry and particularly of Irish miners to serve it in the 1860s, Winchburgh was but a small hamlet at the junction of road and canal, with an inn and staging post. Its setting was rapidly industrialised; road, rail and canal (some good canal bridges nearby). Shale-oil bings dominated it to south and east – that to the south a veritable Table Mountain, one of the biggest bings in Scotland comprising 15 million tonnes, with a footprint of 158 acres. Neat red-brick, late-19th-century miners' rows, in an unusual interlocking L-plan with red sandstone

Above *Niddry Castle*. Right *Miners' rows, Winchburgh*

dressings, were laid out east of the canal, the names chosen from the Hopes of Hopetoun.

Pharmacy, 1904, William Scott
Self-important former police station, a two-and-a-half-storey ashlar, crowstepped edifice in creamy sandstone, dominating a town of single-storey brick. Magnificent dragon's head hopper.

48 **Niddry Castle**, from 15th century
If ever there was a medieval high-rise, it was this. The grim shale-oil black stump etched against a shale bing (the customary view from the train) is entirely misleading, for Niddry has been a place of magnificence, seat of the princely Setons of East Lothian, grand enough to welcome a queen (Mary Queen of Scots stayed here after escaping from Loch Leven). The large L-plan tower-house on its rocky outcrop above the Niddry Burn had a walled cobbled enclosure, round tower at each corner (foundations survive) with stables and ancillary buildings, possibly including a gallery. By the early 17th century, two more storeys had sprouted through the roof in polished ashlar. After centuries of ruin, birdlime and howlets, it has been re-roofed at the 15th-century level, and reoccupied by Peter Wright with the assistance of William A Cadell Architects. The scale of the turnpike stair and of the huge hall (with its chapel), kitchen and adjoining wing, takes you aback. From the hall floor (now a museum), there were two storeys below, and probably four above. Niddry was an enormous, vertically planned mansion of which all we can enjoy today is the plinth. The Historic Scotland decision neither to re-harl or limewash nor to recreate the skyline makes the work seem strangely unfinished. But what an achievement (colour page C8). Large walled

garden to the south-east once the principality of John Reid, the first gardening author in Scottish history, who wrote *The Scots Gardiner* in 1683.

BATHGATE HILLS

49 **Woodcockdale Stables**, *c*.1820, Hugh Baird
Canal-facing rubble cottages and stables, forestairs to both gables, in a tranquil setting. Human accommodation evident; equine accommodation less so. Men above horses.

Avon Aqueduct, *c*.1820, Hugh Baird
The longest and tallest canal aqueduct in Scotland, 246m long and 12 spans 26m high, its masonry arches support a cast-iron trough (colour page C9).

Easter Carriber, late 18th century
Pleasant Improvement farmhouse. Scant remains of 16th-century **Carriber Castle** lie on the banks of the Avon in densely wooded Carriber Glen. Only part of the north gable and the outline of the remaining walls survive. It was built by and for Rab Gibb, stirrup man to the King (under Master of the Royal Stables, Sir James Hamilton of Finnart) and sometime court jester to James V, who was granted the estate of Carriber for his services to the king. He married Margaret Shaw, a royal mistress.

50 **Williamscraigs**, 1878
Rubbly baronial L-plan villa crammed with

Top *Avontoun House (demolished): a splendid design by John Baxter.*
Above *Avon aqueduct.*
Left *Woodcockdale Stables*

Encouraged by James V to swap roles with him, Rab Gibb, when acting King, is said to have feigned boredom with fawning lackeys and courtiers: *awa, awa ye greedy loons, and bring me here my ain true and trusty friend Rab Gibb, the only man in my court who serves from stark love and kindness*. The phrase *for stark love and kindness* was subsequently often to be found on wedding and engagement rings.

Williamscraigs was where the MacKinnon family kept the secret recipe of Drambuie which was entrusted to them by Bonnie Prince Charlie before he left Scotland in 1746. The recipe, produced at the family distillery at Kirkliston, is still what gives the liqueur its unique flavour.

Williamscraigs

furious Scots detail – a hungry crowstepped dormer window, spikily conical roof to a tower. Entrance beneath a spurious reproduction of the great entrance to Fyvie Castle. Splendid **garden pavilion**, hexagonal and weatherboarded, with projecting Gothic window bays and curious clerestory.

Belsyde House

RCAHMS

Craigmailing Hill (or Witches Craig) was one of several locations (others being Hilderstone Hill, and the Knock) where religious conventicles were wont to be held in the late 17th century. The **preaching stone**, a natural boulder on the eastern side of the hill, is inscribed: *On 14th January 1738, there was preached the first sermon by the most worthy Mr Hunter, 37th Chapter of Ezekiel and the 26th verse.* Part of the farm of Lower Craigmailing was used as a Secession Church before the new one was built in Linlithgow in 1806.

51 **Belsyde House**, *c.*1780
Small classical house with flanking single-storey wings and Venetian windows that recall the work of Samuel Bell in Dundee (see *Dundee* in this series). Arms of the Duke of Hamilton lie on the west gable. Sundials on the corners. Gothic lodge.

Wairdlaw Limekilns, 1827
Two draw kilns, with barrel-vaulted access tunnel; built of whinstone with sandstone dressings, 50ft long and 27ft high.

Kipps: detail of the quality of stonework in the circular stair-tower: the rubble would have been harled

Jaques

52 **Kipps**, early 17th century
Ruins of a three-storey château, circular stair-tower at north-east angle and a rectangular one to south-west, in a commanding site overlooking the valley between Cockleroy and Bowdenhill. Home of Sir Robert Sibbald, 17th-century naturalist and antiquary, who relished its *distance from any other seat of the gentry, so that it is a perfect solitude and without the ornaments of art, which other seats have, but has commendable advantages by nature's free gift.*

Bathgate Hills
Stretching from Linlithgow to Bathgate, and virtually to Ecclesmachan in the east, this landscape of great natural beauty offers

wonderful views over the whole of central Scotland and comprises largely empty lands with prehistoric burial grounds, standing stones, pre-Reformation ecclesiastical buildings and sites, with a liberal scattering of towers and châteaux. A landscape of the Covenanters who made slopes their churches and standing stones their pulpits (colour page C4).

Left *Looking north, West Drumcross, Bathgate Hills.* Top *A-framed chalets at Craigs, in the Bathgate Hills.* Above *The château at Lochcote, as drawn by Timothy Pont in 1892.*

Beecraigs Country Park
The Country Park inhabits Beecraigs Wood, with loch and fish farm (the Riccarton Burn first dammed by First World War German prisoners). Modern forestry, conifers, wall-lined birch and beech avenues, archery grounds, fishing, nature trails, and a deer park. Timber **information centre** and **restaurant**, 1991, West Lothian District Council, low-slung and unobtrusive.

Lochcote
In a natural loch to the north of the present reservoir an Iron Age crannog was discovered in the 19th century. No trace above ground of the large 16th-century château depicted by Timothy Pont: nearby fragment consists of a small vaulted chamber, probably a relic of the mansion described in 1807 as showing *baronial gloom and splendour*.

Cairnpapple
The most important mainland archaeological site in Scotland, Cairnpapple was a centre of worship and burial for over 3000 years. First the burial ground, then a henge of 24 large stones, and then an enormous cairn; in all five phases of ritual burial and cremations, with

Cockleroy, an odd name for a hill, has given rise to many legends, most relating to James V's marital infidelities, e.g. *cuckold-le-Roy*. The reality may be more curious. In the 1530s, the French Ambassador brought to James V the order of St Michael, France's highest chivalric order, which was presented to him in Linlithgow. The term then used in Scots was that the King was awarded the *Order of the Golden Cockle*; and perhaps it was accompanied by a hat that resembled the shape on the skyline. Alternatively, it could have been Scots-Gaelic for *Red hood* – cochall (hood) and ruadh (red).

Top *Cathlaw*. Middle *Jubilee Fountain*. Right *The Square*. Above *St John's UF*

concentric rings of pits, ditching and banking. Excavated 1947 (colour page C10). *Open to the public, guidebook available*

53 **Cathlaw**, probably 18th century
Handsomely uneven harled mansion, stone window-dressings, ashlar chimneystacks but curiously harled dormer windows. Its present form *c.*1840, but the unevenness implies something older. Exquisite late-medieval fragments, possibly from Edinburgh's St Giles, adorn the walls.

54 **TORPHICHEN**
Situated on a sheltered plain, away from all post-roads or thoroughfares, and once a place of great importance as it is of high antiquity, it now consists of only a few cottages, and has a straggling and deserted appearance. Thus Torphichen in 1843. Fortune has come to the village with the motorcar, as the luscious, wooded west-facing slope overlooking much of central Scotland has become an object of desire for commuters. The natural focus is the octagonal **Jubilee Fountain**, 1897, in the centre of the village, known as **The Square**, flanked by unpretentious harled or whinstone houses and cottages. The dark-edged white-harled **Torphichen Inn** has been greatly extended beyond its original simplicity. Note the bay windows of **Glebe House** and **Rock Cottages**, 1963, by Reiach & Hall, in harling with timber panels.

St John's UF, Manse Road, 1843
One of the earliest stone-built free kirks built after the Disruption in 1843; sloping shouldered aisles declining on either side of the entrance tower, sadly lacking belfry.

Torphichen Preceptory, 13th-15th century
Curious and atmospheric relic; the crossing and two transepts of the only house of the Knights Hospitallers of St John of Jerusalem in Scotland. The vanished choir may never have been built: the parish kirk occupies the site of

the nave. Traces of domestic offices, refectory and cloister remain on the north. In 1843, *fragments of old massive buildings in the village and the stones in the fences over the face of the adjacent country (indicated) how great and magnificent a seat of population once surrounded the church.* Atmospheric interior, currently gaunt and plain, its plaster having being stripped off. Exquisite traceried windows, one in each transept, and ribbed vaulting to transept and crossing, fine carved archway in the latter, with tomb recess and piscina in the south transept. Reached by turnpike are three upper domestic rooms (complete with fireplaces) devoted to an exhibition of the Knights Hospitallers (colour pages C3, C9).

Left Torphichen Preceptory & Parish Kirk. Top Late-medieval window tracery. Above Gravestone in the kirkyard

Torphichen Parish Kirk, 1756

Neatly scaled T-plan kirk with scrolled skewputts and birdcage belfry: three lofts within, each reached independently, one from a picturesque forestair in the angle. Grey and white interior with elegantly coved and corniced ceiling. Original bar pews – with reserved stalls for the knights, headed by the Prior of Scotland. The heraldic achievements on the two balcony fronts are those of Walter Lord Torphichen and Walter Gillon of Wallhouse. A plaque to Henry Bell (1767-1820), designer of the *Comet* (Europe's first steam-powered ship), born at nearby Torphichen Mill, is under the balcony. 1772 **gatehouse** in the peaceful kirkyard, several fine table tombs, and a **sanctuary stone**. Such stones once sat at a mile radius on each point of the compass, of which the **Gormyre Stone** to the east-north-east and the **Westfield Stone** survive.

The Order of St John was introduced into Scotland by David I in 1153. In 1298, Sir William Wallace held his last convention of barons at Torphichen, and, ironically, it was here that Edward I, Hammer of the Scots, came to pass the night after the Battle of Falkirk later that year. The last Preceptor, Sir James Sandilands, resigned his lands to the Crown in 1563, and was allowed to buy them back at vast cost as a temporal barony, with the title of Lord Torphichen, his seat being at Calder House (see p.98).

Wallhouse elevation

W A Cadell

55 **Wallhouse**, *c.*1840

Romantic, castellated mansion amidst hills and trees, with generally incredible two-dimensional Gothic frontage with octagonal stairs, Gothic windows, crenellations and tall chimneystacks. Built for the Gillon family (arms in the gable above the porch), reclothed by James Maitland Wardrop in 1855. A large stained glass-window within depicts the medieval master of Torphichen. **Doocot**, 1840, lies, ruined, to the north-east. Luscious stonework.

Bridge: Below As it was in 1807. Right As it is today. Middle The entrance façade. Bottom Brig House

Couston, ?early 17th century

Precarious ivy-clad fragment of mansion of the Sandilands, abutting North Couston Farm.

McKean

RCAHMS

T E Gray

56 **Bridge**, from 15th century

Tall, L-plan mansion of the regality of Ogilface, arising dramatically on the west side of wooded Barbauchlaw Burn. Begun as a tower, it was extended south (that wing truncated to a single bay). A round stair-tower in the angle corbelled to square above, rising up to the tower's parapet walk: the 17th-century wing has no parapet. Much, and prettily, extended *in seriatum* in 1886 by Brown & Wardrop; new entrance through a pedimented Gothic porch, with an entire spread of outbuildings. **Brig House** was its dower-house. Seemingly 19th-century, this U-plan harled, crowstepped house, 1582 on porch and a 1656 lintel (west wing, 1900), is certainly earlier.

Brodies

Fooks

RCAHMS

Jaques

Gowanbank (colour page C10)

57 **Gowanbank**, 1842-62, Sir James Gowans
James Gowans' seat. Re-casting of a plain,
*c.*1820 farmhouse belonging to the architect's
mason-father, Walter Gowans. Extended into a
tight U-plan and transformed in character.
Plain roof modulated by rows of hungry corbels,
tall ashlar chimneystacks and a gradual change
in stone from coarse masonry to random rubble.

The **steading, cartshed, dairy** and **cottage**
are in more mature Gowans; panelled façade, the
rubble completely variegated, different coloured,
each stone in its allotted bed. Chimneys random
rubble within panelling. Chamfered corner
windows, stone used for stringcourses and other
details is not polished ashlar but left rude and
hungry. The house at the east end of the byre
bears the inscription *Heb III:4 – For every house
is builded by some man; but he that built all
things is God. Eccles, II:4 1 August 1862.*
Gowans' rigorous 2ft module underpins
everything. Restored as five houses by William A
Cadell Architects & Douglas Davidson Architect.

Sir James Gowans (1821-90) was
born in Blackness. His father, a
working mason, became
quarrymaster, and his son owner or
lessee of most of the principal
quarries in Scotland. A railway and
tramway pioneer, he was knighted
in 1886 for his work in organising
the 1886 Edinburgh International
Exhibition. Lord Dean of Guild of
the City of Edinburgh, he was the
nearest equivalent that Victorian
Edinburgh produced to the great
Glaswegian entrepreneurs.
Although trained as an architect in
David Bryce's office, he was equally
preoccupied with commerce,
railways, quarries and local
government (see *Edinburgh* and
Dundee in this series).

53

Bedlormie Mains

Jaques

ARMADALE TO BROXBURN

The A89, described in 1804 as *the newest and most frequented road between Glasgow and Edinburgh* (later known as *The Great Road*), forms the axis of the 19th-century Texas of Scotland.

Bedlormie Mains, 17th century

Long, white, L-plan house, decapitated stair-tower in the angle: faint echo of Old Bedlormie acquired by Sir Alexander Livingston of Ogilface, shrunk by at least a storey, the ground floor opened out like a later farmhouse, under a shallow 19th-century roof.

58 BLACKRIDGE

A beached mining community, Blackridge stretches in linear fashion along the A89. Beyond **Westcraigs Hills** lies the bleak expanse or *black ridge* of Blawhorn Moss, from which it derived its name. The 1839 **church** is a Gothic-windowed, brown, whinstone God-box, now a house. **Church of Scotland**, 1901, by J G Fairley, is douce with rectangular margined windows surmounted by a tapering slab belfry, cross at apex. **Blackridge Library**, 1974, Haswell-Smith & Partners, is a white curved-cornered book chest on brick stilts; continuous glazed clerestory and swirling, harled curving staircase down to the lower level.

Haswell-Smith & Partners

Jaques

Top *Blackridge Library*. Above *Craig Inn*

Craig Inn, Westcraigs, *c.*1790

Former temple to coaching. Huge three-storey inn, substantial hostelry. Stringcourse, confident symmetry of the façade, huge central bay with three-part windows above an enormous corniced and Doric-pilastered recessed porch. Coach traffic gone, harling picked off, ashlar delaminating: stables behind, entered through cylindrical gate-piers with domed tops. To be housing and museum to coaching.

59 ARMADALE

Sir William Honeyman of Graemsy, Lord Armadale (named after a property he had inherited in Sutherland), lent his name to the locality when he became landlord, *c.*1800 – a hamlet servicing travellers (with *a very considerable private school*) until the industrial boom created the *Dale*. **St Paul's Episcopal Chapel**, 1858, indicates the early leanings of incoming workers. By 1912, the town had coalfields, whinstone quarries, steelworks, and brick, tile and fire-brick yards. The wide central road and extended pavement defeats any attempt to provide a central focus. Long and linear, isolated monuments or industrial relics punctuate a low-slung environment stretching along Main Street.

The Cross
Centre of the town. Two older hostelries vie for custom over the cast-iron **Kerr Memorial**, 1919. On the north-east, the **Star Hotel**, possibly late 18th century, coaching entrance to Main Street now blocked, is long, low and turns the corner in a crisp white, c.1850, entrance. The black-and-white **Hunting Lodge**, crisply quoined with stringcourse, is c.1840.

Council Office, Main Street, 1966, J A W Grant
Entered through a timber-mullioned curtain-wall into a hall separating offices from the taller, harled council chamber with a flagpole. **St Helen's Place**, South Street, 1966, by Roberts & Paul, a three-storey stepped terrace of houses above shops at the ground floor, has each house with a large window and balcony gazing southwards. The crisp vision of bright, sunny contemporary life is now somewhat smudged.

The Goth, Main Street, 1911, Thomas Roberts Originally The Gothenburg, it is Armadale's most distinctive landmark, designed for the Armadale Public House Society (dedicated to curbing alcoholic excess), based on the Swedish improved-pub model. Stained-glass windows and extensive columned interior added, 1924, by Peddie & Kinnear, followed by a curiously leaning stone clock tower (not unlike that of a Scottish tolbooth) with an arcaded ground floor and louvred octagonal cap in late art nouveau. It was erected in memory of Malcolm Mallace, President of the Society.

The Kerr Memorial commemorates Mrs Elizabeth Kerr of Dunolly Cottage who *near this spot, 26 Nov. 1919, was fatally injured in saving a child from being run over by a passing motor car – Unbounded courage and compassion joined. Erected by the public of Armadale.*

Kerr Memorial

*The so-called **Gothenburg system** was designed to discourage drinking to excess, food or coffee being offered as a ready alternative. In 1895 British critics of the system unkindly pointed out that Gothenburg, with a population considerably smaller than that of Dundee, had four times as many drunkards as the Scottish city.*
R Kenna & A Mooney, *People's Palaces*, 1983

The Goth

East Main Street
Miners' Welfare Institute, 1923
That it has the grandeur of a town hall symbolises the importance of mining to Armadale: a clever re-use of 17th-century motifs, crowstepped central bay and three-storey tower with corbelled balustraded flat above.

Academy Street
In the urban sense, there are no real streets in Armadale; simply an adjacency of buildings. Comfortingly solid and sedate **Parish Church**, *c.*1870, with neat belfry and pedimented porch. The **Primary** & **Nursery Schools**, 1878-1911, occupy the former Academy; symmetrical, two gables crowned with thistles flank a projecting central block. Fine double-storey halls with hammer-beam roofs and first-floor galleries. **Armadale Academy**, 1967, by J A W Grant, is even more austere; curtain-walled geometric blocks, floor-to-ceiling mullioned windows, hall framed by orange brickwork.

St Anthony's, Greig Crescent, 1977, Haswell-Smith & Partners
Sympathetically ground-hugging primary school with chocolate-coloured walls, deep fascia and rooflights at the centre: each classroom identified by a projecting hexagon.

Top Hall, Armadale Primary School. *Above* St Anthony's. *Below* Bathgate: proposed Town House. It is unclear whether this was ever built

60 **BATHGATE**
Fast up, fast down – or has Bathgate more staying power? Source of the 19th-century Scots oil boom, Bathgate was an ancient market centre of a fertile parish *covered with thriving plantations which tend generally to heighten the beauty of the landscape and improve the climate.* Formerly an ancient sheriffdom (one of its sheriffs was Sir James Hamilton of Finnart), it was erected a burgh of barony in 1661 with seven annual (mostly cattle) fairs. The royal castle was gifted by Robert Bruce to his daughter Marjorie who, after marrying Walter the High Steward, founded the Royal House of Stewart. Earthworks still identifiable in the golf course. The old town lay on the lower slopes of the Bathgate Hills on the edge of the policies of Balbardie House, seat of the Marjoribanks of that Ilk. The old Glasgow Road went up Cochrane Street into Main Street, and left up Shuttle Row to Torphichen, or to Drumcross and Edinburgh up Hopetoun Street. The Old Parish Church, at Kirkton, lay to the south-east.

56

Bathgate Chemical Works, looking like Fort Apache

After 1824, its streets were to be paved and lit by gas, there was to be a weekly market on Wednesdays, and a police system was to be introduced. That market became the *central cornmarket for West Lothian and the adjoining counties*. By 1843, change was in the air: *The town now consists of two parts, the old and the new. The old town is built on a steep ridge, and the streets are narrow and crooked. The new town is built on a regular plan, and has a good appearance. Within these few years, the town has been considerably extended: there has also been a large increase of population, which is principally supported by the weaving of cotton goods for the Glasgow manufacturers, and by the lime and coalworks in the vicinity.* The character of the burgh changed from being very rustic to fashionable; new streets – Mid Street, Marjoribanks Street, Engine Street flourished; as did the principal cross axis of North Bridge Street and Hopetoun Street.

In the mid-19th century, the economic focus shifted decisively southwards to Hopetoun Street and George Street. The relocation of the ancient kirk from Kirkton to Main Street in 1739, and its replacement by the present High Kirk, facing Jarvey Street in 1882, did not stop the trend. Industrial Bathgate moved inexorably southwards becoming posher as it spread: the Steelyard (named after the steelyard or public weighing machine) became George Place, and Engine Street became George Street. That is now the pedestrianised centre of the town, and liberally punctuated with brick planters and trees. 1992 environmental art in Steelyard Square based on local themes by Sibylle von Halen, Lynn Clarke & Robert Hutcheson (Peter McGowan Associates, Landscape Architects) (colour page C10).

⁶¹ George Place

Reception area to Bathgate from the east, fronted on the north side by the **Royal Hotel**, *c.*1840, with its quoins and balustrade, probably an aggrandisement of an earlier building. The **Emporium Building**, *c.*1870,

At Whiteside, off Whitburn Road, James *Paraffin* Young, nicknamed *Lord of the Oils* by his friends, opened the world's first oil refinery in 1848. Whilst in England, he had been informed by a college friend that the coal mine at Boghead by Torbanehill, beside Bathgate, spluttered like a parrot when burning and gave a light as clear as any candle – earning it a nickname *parrot* or *cannel* coal. Young discovered that the coal from this mine, when heated, oozed with oil. He established the soon immensely profitable Bathgate Chemical Works to exploit it (much to the annoyance of the feu superior who thought he was simply mining coal). Young later discovered that West Lothian shale was likewise oil-bearing. There were soon refineries at Broxburn, Pumpherston (Livingston), Oakbank (East Calder) and Uphall. Shale was mined, broken up into lumps, tipped into retorts and heated. It produced gas, crude oil, ammonia water and spent shale, which was deposited in huge pink mounds. The many products from shale included naphtha, burning oils, lubricating oils, solid paraffin, soft paraffin, sulphate of ammonia (for fertiliser) and, lastly, petrol. Approximately one-fifth of a total resource of 200 million tonnes of shale has so far been worked: the balance remains below ground.

Old Bathgate, prior to its demolition

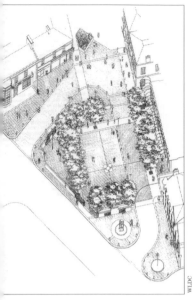

Above *The Steelyard, Bathgate, with its environmental improvements.*
Right *Clydesdale Bank*

St David's Church: original perspective

T R Irvine, gives scale to the corner of Whitburn Road at Grieg's Corner in the manner of a typical mid-century market building; giant Ionic colonnade facing Whitburn Road, Ionic-pilastered pavilions flanking the corner and wings with, above, a curiously balustraded attic storey over the cornice. Once restored, it will be classy indeed. **Clydesdale Bank**, 1913, built by W T Oldrieve as the post office, is particularly distinguished Scots Revival; harled, stone margins, fine dormer windows, corner turret and carved entrance doorway. **Dreadnought Hotel**, Whitburn Road, 1901, J G Fairley, somewhat heavyweight baronial in the manner of a commercial hotel, crowstepped gables, bay windows and pedimented entrance. The nearby **Social Work Department**, 1988, Campbell & Arnott, a sprightly courtyard in buff brick and red pantiles, presents twin Italianate gables to the roundabout, with colourful yellow lintels, blue and green steel trim to its lofty, pedimented, entrance canopy.

[62] **St David's Church**, George Street, 1904, J G Fairley
Outstanding, vertically proportioned church, its attenuated, slender tower rocketing into the sky capped by an ogee dome. Everything is designed to emphasise verticality; slender lancets of the entrance tower and the prettily scaled adjacent hall. Fine, open, timber-roofed interior, gallery the one side, aisle the other. Stained glass celebrating mining and engineering, 1954, W Wilson.

Woolworths, *c*.1928
In stone rather than the customary faience, with chevron mouldings above the first-floor windows. **111 George Street**, *c*.1978, West Lothian Architects, is a striking insertion: a

glazed first floor billows out on concrete
columns above a recessed ground floor.

South Bridge Street
The old turnpike road, and one reason why the
old town moved south. The railway impinges at
King Street which used to be called Engine
Knowe, where three rival hostelries –
Bathgate Inn, **Commercial Inn** and
Railway Tavern fight it out for custom.
Lothian & Borders Police Headquarters,
1958, by T B Gibson & Laing is a prettily
scaled building of its time – projecting porch
canopy with George & Dragon motif by
Norman Forrest above; curtain-walled within a
thin brick frame but set back and
underscaled for its setting. Confident red
sandstone baroque on the gusset of **North
Bridge Street**, 1912, by T R Irvine, with oriel,
projecting bay window, ball finials and a
pedimented entrance.

63 **West Lothian District Council Offices**,
1976, Roberts & Paul
Handsome free-standing sculpture in white
marble, stone, riven slate and exposed
aggregate panels. (Former burgh) chamber
cantilevered out on piloti beneath a pavilion
roof, the town's shield proudly displayed on the
slate-clad gable. Good extension, 1987,
completing the courtyard in crisp blockwork,
tall round-headed corner window, similar
window facing into the court. Mounded soft
landscaping completes.

64 **Regal Cinema**, 1938, J R McKay
Regal indeed; a symmetrical design in
roughcast and artificial stone, stair pavilions
on either side mounting to an art deco
pediment and flagpole. Fine floral stained glass
in the first-floor foyer.

65 **Hopetoun Street**
The principal thoroughfare through Bathgate

*Left Social Work Department,
Whitburn Road. Top St David's
Church. Middle District Council
Offices. Above Proposed Kinema by
J R McKay, on the other side of the
street from the one that was built*

Above *Regal Cinema*. Right *Royal Bank of Scotland before its evisceration*

which, joined to North Bridge Street, forms the old road from Armadale to Edinburgh, the boundary between 19th-century Bathgate and the older town to the north. Traces of former prosperity and gentility survive – **52**, with its recessed Doric porch, pilasters and fluted lintel, and the two fine pilastered doors of **Whyte's Bar**.

The junction with George Street, once graced by the cast-iron McLagan fountain (now re-erected in the Steelyard – its removal led to the nickname of *the fountain-less cross*), was greeted by a widening marked by a splendid curving corner **Royal Bank of Scotland**, with corniced windows, balustraded porch and great chimneystack; now truncated, all detail cloured off, leaving neutered windows gaping through chocolate-coloured harl. The **New Royal Bar**, at the junction of North Bridge Street, has a fine consoled and pedimented corner door. **Bank of Scotland**, *c.*1950, an elegant essay in late 1930s classical, has stair-tower at one end graced by flagpole, leading to two plain office storeys above.

St John's, Mid Street, 1895, by William Tennant, is a confident Gothic barn with tall broach spire. **Health Centre**, 1976, West Lothian County Council Architects, comprises chunky geometric shapes of granite-block plinth with ribbed concrete superstructure, like a squared-off roof. Fortress health. Just east lies the neo-Georgian brick façade of the **Swimming Pool**, *c.*1935. **Minara Place** is a handsome Victorian corner block with its name in a quoined roundel.

Bennie Museum, 9-11 Mansfield Street, late 18th century
One of the last remaining rows of single-storey superior stone cottages of old Bathgate, with an ashlar façade and chimneys and red

pantiles with typical slate apron. Converted to museum specialising in local history.

66 Livery Street
Church of the Immaculate Conception, 1885

Soaring confection on the site of the 1822 Seceders' Kirk, the west façade framed by twin pinnacles focused upon a twin entrance, heavily cusped and carved in ashlar. Large aisled church within, a rich Gothic sanctuary, possibly 1908, by Charles Menart. Altar of Sienna marble. *Baptism of Christ* window in the baptistry, 1959, by William Wilson. **Livery Street** houses and cottages were largely redeveloped, from 1977, by Gordon Duncan Somerville. Three-storey harled and slated flats and houses with excellent landscaping, rather vernacular in such a town centre location. Compare Roberts & Paul's 1960s flats in Marjoribanks Street, and Wilson & Wilson's 1950s flats in Drumcross Road.

Church of the Immaculate Conception

Left Jarvey Street, c.1910.
Below Masonic Lodge

67 Jarvey Street

Possibly named after a French Huguenot family named Jarves, which fled to Scotland in the late 17th century to escape religious persecution. Jarvey Street, now in sad decline, is Bathgate's most historic, almost like a close to the High Kirk.

Masonic Lodge, 1902, Peter Henderson
A small two-storey building utterly distinguished by its splendid central doorway and ornate, curving, oriel window with small, leaded panes of glass. Shops at ground floor; Ladbroke's unsympathetic, Davidson's excellent. Adjacent **Bathgate Co-operative Society**, 1902, Peter Henderson, dominated by three ornamental gables.

High Kirk, Jarvey Street

James Young Simpson (1811-70) was born in Bathgate, the eighth child of a baker. Very much the traditional Scottish *lad o' pairts*, he studied first arts, then medicine in Edinburgh becoming a member of the Royal College of Surgeons in 1830 (when only 19) and given the Chair of Midwifery in 1840 (when only 29). In 1845 he bought the house in Queen Street from which he practised. Following experiments with both mesmerism and ether to relieve the pain of childbirth, he took up the suggestion of David Waldie in Linlithgow that chloroform might be the answer. Finding it to be successful, Simpson demonstrated its use to his medical colleagues in 1847. Despite bitter attacks from those who maintained that pain was good for their character, chloroform gained the seal of approval when Queen Victoria used it at the birth of one of her sons. Knighted in 1866 and loaded with honours from many countries, he died at Queen Street in May 1870. He was buried in Warriston Cemetery, his widow having refused the offer of burial in Westminster Abbey. It was said that *Simpson adopted obstetrics when it was the lowest and most ignoble of the medical arts; he has left it a science numbering among its professors many of the most distinguished of our modern physicians.*

Corn Exchange, 1857
Symbol of the agricultural prosperity of the parish, this handsome quoined building, with its keystoned windows and balustraded roof, was built as an agricultural auction rooms. Now mutilated into nightclub mode. Adjacent **shop**, *c.*1935, particularly fine in black marble, curving stone and horizontal windows.

68 **High Kirk**, 1882, Wardrop & Reid
Pinnacled English Gothic kirk tower with Romanesque details, and Romanesque windows. Horseshoe gallery. Atmospheric graveyard with many fine memorials.

69 **Main Street**
All that remains of this historic Bathgate street, where Sir James Young Simpson (discoverer of the anaesthetic properties of chloroform) was born in 1811, is the plan and the **Star Inn**, *c.*1860, a handsome black-and-white L-plan hostelry. **Simpson Memorial Church**, 1979, by Ian McMillan consists of curved harled walls at odds with the regiment of vertical windows on their brick plinths. The **Glenman's Tavern**, probably 18th century, is a white, substantial inn, with stone margins, good doorway and wallhead chimney.

70 **St Columba's Episcopal**, Glasgow Road, 1916, W J Walker Todd
Curious, harled, little church with squat tower, semi-octagonal sanctuary and arched doorway. Apple-slice tile decoration to the concrete lintels.

71 **Windyknowe Primary School**, 1963, Alison & Hutchison & Partners
Assembly hall has eye-catching hyperbolic paraboloid roof supporting a black-mullioned curtain-wall, on four slender chamfered concrete buttresses like outstretched fingers.

72 **Boghead**
The home of the Robertson-Durham family, demolished 1962, leaving a **lodge**, with a hood-moulded window, and a roofless rectangular **doocot**. It was on this estate that Torbanehill *cannel* coal was first mined by Paraffin Young for extracting mineral oil. **Whiteside** was the site of Paraffin Young's first oil refinery in 1848. The **Shovel Works**, Mill/Easton Roads, is a rare survival; dense, urban, Victorian, small factory-works with two-storey curved brick corner. Still makes forestry shovels.

73 Balbardie House, 1793, Robert Adam
(demolished)
Built for Alexander Marjoribanks, Balbardie
was Robert's last villa, set in an outstandingly
beautiful landscape. The central block a storey
higher, with steeply pitched roof, the
pedimented and pilastered first floor was
linked to its pavilions by two outstanding
exedra (concave-vaulted porches). The
Balbardie coal mine tunnelled underneath.
Once the Marjoribanks abandoned it, it became
occupied by miners then demolished in 1956
following subsidence. Recollected in **Balbardie
Park**, with its long, yellow, metal-clad **Sports
Centre**, 1987 (colour page C11).

Windyknowe Primary School

Left *Exedra at Balbardie House
(demolished). Compare the design
with Adam's proposed entrance to
Champfleurie* (see page 42).
Below *Houses rising up the hill
in Bathgate.* Bottom *Balbardie
Primary School*

74 Balbardie Primary School,
Torphichen Street, 1904, J G Fairley
Well-proportioned and elegantly detailed school
with separate *boys* and *girls* entrance porches
flanking their respective wings. Stringcourses,
armorial panels and elegantly proportioned
gabled roofline.

Marjoribanks Street, named after Alexander
Marjoribanks of Balbardie, who became
Bathgate's first Provost after the 1824 Act. As

Bathgate Academy was endowed by John Newlands, a carpenter who emigrated from Bathgate to Jamaica, where he made his fortune as a plantation owner. On his death in 1799, he left most of his money to *erect a free school in the parish of Bathgate*. Unfortunately, his will was disputed by relatives (exactly the same story as the Morgan Hospital in Dundee – see *Dundee* in this series) and his wishes were not implemented until some 30 years later, and then with only one-third of his fortune. His name is commemorated annually in the Newlands Day procession, with its tradition of building triumphal arches of clipped green spruce in the main streets of Bathgate; and in the Newlands Oration given on the steps of the Academy.

normal, the quality in Bathgate moved uphill for better views and absence of smoke. The higher, the better; some excellent Victorian villas of all shapes and sizes. **Wellpark**, *c*.1860, now the District Library Headquarters, was built as the home of the Wolfes (owners of the shovel factory), coursed stone with swelling two-storey semicircular bay in ashlar. Fine plasterwork within.

75 **Bathgate Academy**, 1833, R & R Dickson Particularly distinguished late-neoclassical school. Logically planned around two courtyards, on each side of the hall – which acts as entrance pavilion suitably graced with Doric columns (for learning) and capped by a gracious belfry. Flanking Doric colonnade to comparable but low side pavilions with blank windowless gables. Now part of **West Lothian College of Further Education** (colour page C11).

Above *Bathgate Academy, c.1900.*
Below *Telephone Exchange, Balbardie Road, as originally built, c.1956*

WLDC Libraries

WLDC

Cloisterfield, Balbardie Road, by the same architect as Wellpark (to judge from the semicircular bay window), has an art nouveau doorway and a red tiled roof. **Grange Hill**, 1904, is more austere – two full storeys of crisp stonework, windows of the *c*.1900 variety and oversailing eaves. A splendid group of modern stepped, pitched-roof **villas**, brick plinths, harled gables sweeping up Balbardie Street, getting the best view over Bathgate.

76 **St Mary's Academy** & **Lindsay High School**, 1931, T Aikman Swan Educational barracks guarding the Edinburgh entrance to Bathgate, one for each religious

denomination, with modulated corner, great stair window, chimney and portholes.

[77] **Salt Cellar**, 1988, Lothian Regional Council
Eye-catching whitish dome 41m across, 13m high, constructed (at second attempt) by spraying concrete over an inflatable shape, the latter flown in from Pittsburgh, USA.

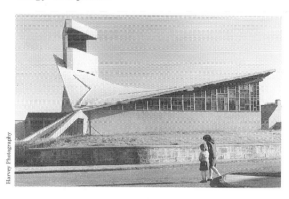

Left Old Parish Kirk from the air.
Top Cloisterfield. Above Salt Cellar

[78] **Old Parish Kirk**, Kirkton
Gaunt rectangular ruin originally belonging to Newbattle Abbey, abandoned 1739 when the High Kirk was built in Main Street. Vestigial capitals to its wide doorway, and lancet window on the north side. Turfed within, and lined with memorial tablets to the Newlands, Marjoribanks and other Bathgate worthies. Notable, if badly weathered, recumbent 13th-century stone effigy of a priest.

The Covenanter's Memorial, 1673, a recumbent slab beautifully maintained and edged with flowers states:
Here lies the body of James Davie, who was shot at Blackdub, April 1673 by Heron
For his adhering to the word of God And Scotland's covenanted word of Reformation
In opposition to popery, prelacy, perjury and tyranny

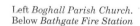

[79] **Boghall Parish Church**, 1965,
Wheeler & Sproson
Hyperbolic paraboloid roof soaring like wings above glazing which sits on a harled plinth.

Left Boghall Parish Church.
Below Bathgate Fire Station

[80] **Bathgate Fire Station**, Starlaw Roundabout, Boghall, 1991, Lothian Region Architects
Stepped-back cutaway rotunda, each step back providing clerestory light deeper into the

Above *Easter Inch*. Right *Motorola*

centre of the plan, the apex providing toplight into the muster bay.

Easter Inch, 1869
Over-the-top farm steading, entered through a Gothic arch. Within, round corbelled-out – to square plinth rising up to a tall corbelled tower with oriel windows and spiky cap (colour page C11).

81 **Motorola Headquarters**, Easter Inch, 1991, Robert Matthew Johnson-Marshall & Partners
Enormous (speedily built) high-tech manufacturing plant in the form of interlocking rectangles, solid blockwork contrasting with transparent curtain-walling, excellent landscaping, and gracious curtain-walled entrance with oversailing canopy like a porte-cochère. Elegant, if spartan, geometric design. Public art lines the motorway: the **Saw Tooth Ramps** are five rigidly shaped pyramid hills of green grass, in a clever echo of Five Sisters bing at West Calder, designed by Patricia Leighton; Carter McGlyn, Landscape Architects.

Refuse Disposal Depot, 1984, West Lothian District Council Architects
Working sleek silver-metal garage for dustbin lorries; scarlet-metal, round-edged stair-tower and restroom like a bookend.

82 **Bangour Village Hospital**, 1896-1906, Hippolyte J Blanc
Originally a lunatic asylum for the City of Edinburgh, on the pioneering German-inspired vision of civilised treatment for the mentally ill, on the hilly and beautiful estate of the Hamiltons of Bangour, at one time with its own railway station and shop. During the First

Bangour Village Hospital from the air

World War, injured servicemen could be shipped direct here from the Channel ports. During the 1930s, Bangour became a tuberculosis sanatorium, fresh air and food from its own home farm being important to recuperation.

Village Church, 1924-30, H O Tarbolton
Possibly the largest 20th-century church in Lothian outside Edinburgh, grandly sited like a garrison chapel. Huge buttressed west gable, traceried Romanesque windows, dominated by a stumpy rectangular tower with a lead-clad broach spire. Apsidal **War Memorial Chapel** to south, choir and vestry with small tower to north. Interior fashioned from sandstone grading to ashlar at the clerestory (much stone from the demolished Hamilton Palace, Lanarkshire). Dark-stained roof of hammer-beams and kingposts, and barrel-vaulted chancel. Church furniture by Tarbolton was carved by the hospital's woodworkers. **The Hall**, 1904, Hippolyte J Blanc, is a large grey stone pile; Venetian in south gable, round-headed dormer windows, square flytower with oasthouse roof. Organ from Lonsdale Cinema, Carlisle.

Bangour Village Church

Nurses' Home porches flanked by two octagonal towers capped with lead ogee roofs. The E-plan **Medical Hospital** has a projecting three-storey turreted entrance.

Elevation of the hospital block

Dechmont House

Dechmont House (demolished) was on an ancient site. Here was where James Young tried to persuade the explorer Dr David Livingstone to buy an estate and settle on the profits of his book, *Missionary Travels and Researches in South Africa*, 1857. Livingstone never settled in Scotland and went back to Africa where he died, as did his wife. The estate was bought, instead, by Young's partner, Edward Meldrum, and the house built in 1863.

Above *Craig Binning*. Right *Houstoun House drawn by its restoring architect, Ian G Lindsay*

Administrative Centre in plain bright harl and red sandstone dressings is vaguely Scots Revival.

Drumcrosshall
Courtyard group of pantiled cottages behind Victorian dormered farmhouse, on a site of some antiquity. At one time a thriving community of blacksmiths, with their own ale shop and general store. The **farm** has an elegant portico with a broken pediment.

83 **Craig Binning**, *c.*1840
Neatly scaled villa, façade Victorianised by an advanced and balustraded bay with porch, decorative quoins, angular ranks of chimneys and scroll terminations to first-floor window margins.

84 **Houstoun House**, Uphall, from 16th century
Striking vertical U-plan mansion, brilliant-white harl, stone margins to windows and doors, and steeply pitched and slated crowstepped roof. It has been through many changes: the skyline probably sliced in the 18th century, additions infilling the square with a new wing and stair to the north-west, causing a re-siting of the entrance first to the south and then to the east. Restored as his home by the architect, Ian G Lindsay, in the 1940s. Subsequently refurbished and extended as hotel by Wheeler & Sproson, 1970, who removed the east porch and added the attractive glazed foyer to the east and

Harvey Photography

sympathetic, slate-hung bedroom block. Normal ground-floor vaulted cellars now bar and meeting room; delightful principal-floor apartments with much of the original panelling and plasterwork. The north wing across the walled courtyard is the **woman house**, 1600, with a **coachhouse**, 1736, and **stables** adjoining. Good 17th-century lectern **doocot**, **sundial**, 1757, on a square baluster, and lovely formal gardens. A most beautiful place, Houstoun was built for, or extended by, the advocate, Sir Thomas Shairp. Further additions are the 1980 crowstepped bedroom block, and flat-roofed private house to the west by Donald McInnes (colour page C12).

A I Hunter

Top *Houstoun House showing the 1980 bedroom block.* Above *Detail*

UPHALL

The two communities of Uphall and Broxburn are distinct, linked only casually by inter-war housing. The Brox Burn (from which the neighbourhood takes its name – a haunt of badgers) crosses to the south side of the *great road* initially, in a deep wooded glen. The older and smarter houses lie south, whereas industry and poorer houses lay north. Many quiet and frequently charming *culs-de-sac*. **West Main Street** enters uphill from the west and a long straggle of single-storey fermtoun cottages line the south side of the street, *c.*1800. **Nos 33 & 35** form two colour-washed semi-detached villas with Doric pilasters. The **Stables** (to Dovehill House, No 33), down in the woods by the burn, is a delightful conversion in part-rubble part-harl by Brian Curry, a huge circular window in its gable. **Millhouse**, down by Miller's Bridge, also by the burnside, has been domesticated; harled and pantiled and turned into a house. **55a & 55b** West Main

Stables, West Main Street

T E Gray

Harvey Photography

Above School Place, as first built. The courtyard form was selected to give a sense of village green to the otherwise linear Uphall. Right Oatridge Hotel

Street, 1984, are by Richard Jaques. Note particularly the half-timbered **pavilion** said to be from the Empire Exhibition, but much more likely the 1911 Glasgow Exhibition.

School Place housing, 1962, Wheeler & Sproson
Specifically designed to attract key workers for industry replacing shale-mining, School Place was about as smart as could be – a crisp, startlingly bright, geometric courtyard of houses and flats distinguished by the slender four-storey block of flats terminating the western corner, with good scale and enclosure. Its brilliance needs maintaining better.

John Cameron

Oatridge Hotel, c.1800
Formerly the *well-known Uphall Inn*, this lovely building is the product of many generations. Examine its golden stonework and where stringcourses start and stop. Three long, spreading bays, projecting pedimented entrance, with handsome and fashionable Regency porch.
Muir's Buildings, West Main Street, 1890, a long two-storey range of flats above shops, has an uneasy mansard roof but pretty pedimented gable with clock and ball finial.

Middleton Hall, from c.1700
Some house. Of the original mansion created by the Revd George Barclay from Strathbrock Castle after retirement from his ministry in the parish, there is little easily identifiable. The Earls of Buchan substantially extended it, possibly in the later 18th century with a delightful south-facing harled façade, projecting entrance bay, stringcourse, pavilion roof etc. Extended rather coarsely, probably by

WLDC Libraries

ROAHMS

Fooks

J McIntyre Henry, *c.*1909, with a new upper storey and wings, as headquarters of Scottish Oils. Fine wall paintings on the stairwell within. Now a residential home for the elderly. Adjacent, delightful wooded estate was developed as a picturesque garden estate for staff of Scottish Oils, *c.*1924.

Ecclesmachan Road
No 9, 1893, is a smart, south-facing, L-plan villa with an excellent ashlar doorway and adjacent window and scrolled gable. **Lindenlea**, No 18a opposite, has a pyramid-roofed projecting bay.

Crossgreen Farm, *c.*1830
Plain Improvement farmhouse in rubble with a pilastered doorway, crying out for harl or limewash to give it the grandeur it deserves. **25-29** Ecclesmachan Road is a row of different dated cottages, some harled, some rubble, some coursed, some pantiled, some slated. The **Wee Hoose**, No 27, was seriously wee – one large door and one wee window – before amalgamation with its neighbour.

Strathbrock St Nicholas,
Ecclesmachan Road, from 12th century A vision of old Scotland on its ancient hilltop graveyard gazing south towards the Pentlands. The original plan was simplicity itself; square tower at the western end (two-storey now capped by a bellcote), long rectangular nave and originally square chancel (now extended). The plan, like so many Scottish kirks, is very Swedish. Of the original 12th-century church, there survive the nave walls, and beautiful south door, with its shafts, scalloped capitals and roll mouldings. Barrel-vaulted **aisle** of the Shairps of Houstoun, *c.*1620, but only a

Left Middleton Hall in 18th-century mode prior to gargantuan extension. *Top* Principal staircase decoration. *Above* Garden village houses. *Below* The Wee Hoose. *Bottom* Strathbrock St Nicholas

Lothian Studio

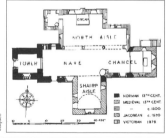

Jaques

Norman south door, Strathbrock St Nicholas

Below *Advertisement for Broxburn petrol.* Bottom *View from the Old Town up to the (demolished) Town Hall, c.1900.* Right *Broxburn oil works*

forestair, 1644, survives of the **Buchan Loft**. The **north aisle**, 1878, is by Wardrop & Reid, who also rebuilt the upper stage of the **tower** and added the belfry. The 1503 bell is from an earlier church. The ground storey of the tower is the burial place of the Earls of Buchan, a wall tablet commemorating Thomas, Lord Erskine, Lord Chancellor of England, and the Hon. Henry Erskine, Lord Advocate of Scotland 1783 and 1806. Stained glass, 1922, by P MacGregor Chalmers and, 1962 by William Wilson (colour page C13).

Tombstones include a table-top Adam & Eve with a tree loaded with apples, and a bronze monument, 1866, by Sir John Steell to Lt-Col. John Drysdale. **Manse**, late 17th century, uphill from the kirk, was built as Uphall House for Katherine, Dowager Lady Cardross. Later over-scaled two-storey hexagonal bay, and much more diminutive Victorian window bay.

BROXBURN
A village on the lands of the Earls of Buchan, with toll house and *good inn* – the early 19th-century **Buchan Arms** – transformed into Shaleopolis by the arrival of the canal in 1821 and the railway in 1849. After the discovery of oil-bearing shale – Raeburn shale, Mungle shale, Broxburn shale, Fells shale, Houston coal and Foote coal – everything was utterly transformed by shale mines, shale bings and oil works and the inevitable miners' rows – the Stewartfield Rows and the Greendykes Rows. Old Broxburn was overwhelmed. The road north to Winchburgh passes a number of reconditioned miners' rows, winding between gigantic pink bings, as though it were Shale Canyon. The centre lies between Binny Place and the turn-off to Winchburgh, marked by one of the older surviving buildings in the town – **Green Tree Tavern**, harled with stone margins, *c.*1800 – and the Buchan Arms.

Apart from the regal survival of **Holmes Farm**, central Broxburn is almost entirely Victorian with modern insertions. The demolished town hall, a large rubbly barn, stood shoulder to the Buchan Arms Hotel facing down Station Road.

Kirkhill House

Kirkhill House, 1590

A fine sight on the hillside, at one time much finer. It has lost a storey and its roofscape, and some bays off the western end. It lies under an 18th-century roof, with probably 19th-century windows at ground level. The entrance to the stair-tower (itself truncated) is a particularly fine moulded doorway. On the eastern gable, there is a remnant at roof level of an elegant ashlar corner pilaster. Built into the steading is a beautiful scrolled dormer-windowhead, and a balustered armorial panel. House and steading converted as flats and houses (colour page C12).

Our Lady's High School, 1969, Alison & Hutchison

Crisp, flat-roofed, geometric shapes comprising courtyard of assembly hall, gymnasium, swimming pool and specialist teaching units. On West Main Street, note the flat-roofed, ruddy-hued **doctors' surgery** on the south side, in the crisp geometry of the 1930s, but with 1950s windows. **Port Buchan**, on the canal, has great potential.

Our Lady's High School

(Former) West Church, 1855

Born a free kirk, now a funeral directors, and grander than most free kirks with excellent stonework, banded, multi-coloured ashlar containing lancet windows rising to a splendid belfry.

73

St John Cantius & St Nicholas, 1880,
Shiells & Thomson
By far the grandest church in Broxburn is the
Catholic kirk which beckons by its slender
spire. General Early English, each chapel along
the aisle has its own gable. Iron shafts with
fluted caps support a steeply pitched roof
within. The 15th- or 16th-century **font** is from
the medieval parish church excavated by
Kirkhill. The rich Gothic **high altar** in Caen
stone and marble is by Pugin & Pugin. **Canon
Hoban Memorial Hall**, 1936, and **Church
Hall**, 1937, by Reginald Fairlie. **Memorial
Chapel**, 1857, to the 12th Earl of Buchan is a
simple but well-detailed Gothic mausoleum
surmounted by a guardian angel.

The **oil works** to the north of Broxburn is
now superseded by an industrial estate.

Windsor Lodge, Main Street, 1856
Architectural minestrone; smart Doric-
columned porch, capped by pedimented window
above, and then a corbelled and gabled parapet
above that; the bay window to the west heavily
crowstepped with a ball finial. Ironwork above
the porch capped by an extraordinary cast-iron
thistle like an angel extending its wings.

The **Library**, 1985, by Bamber & Hall, a flat-
roofed rectangle, with entrance through a cut-
away corner beneath the oversailing roof with
painted timber fascia, has decorated crazy-
paving stonework on the gable.

Buchan Arms Hotel, *c.*1780
End of a long row of substantial two-storey
harled buildings with painted margins and
good chimneystacks.

*Burnside, Broxburn, drawn by
Richard Jaques*

Station Road

Stumpy Victorian corner with blind dormer
window turns into Station Road and down to
the old town; comprehensively redeveloped by
Wheeler & Sproson, 1968, in modern stepped
flats with south-facing living room windows set
back from Station Road and staggered.

*Old Town, Broxburn, as redeveloped
in 1968*

West Burnside

Peaceful enclave on the banks of the Brox
Burn, mainly single-storey cottages and one or
two larger two-storey houses. Burnside
Walkway links Broxburn and Uphall by
way of path and picnic areas.

Station Road and **Almondell Road**, lined
with more substantial Victorian bungalows and
houses. **St Nicholas Free Church**, 1890, by
J C Fairley, has a Gothic frontage with wide
shoulders and good plate-tracery. **Old Post
Office**, c.1880, on the corner of West Burnside,
is a crowstepped corner. **Knysna Bank**, 1885,
has an intriguingly carved florid porch.

Regal, Greendykes Road, 1937,
T Bowhill Gibson
Smart cinema, shallow-pedimented art deco
façade flanked by two flagpoled stair-towers.

District Council Offices, 1988, West Lothian
Department of Architectural Services, presents
a chamfered corner into **Church Street**; brick
plinth, heavy oversailing roof (diminutive
pediment with clock to Main Street), glazing
running as a clerestory beneath the eaves.
Neat contemporary U-plan courtyard housing
in Church Street – blue and red tiles, orange
brick, porches and dormer windows.

Broxburn Parish Church, East Main Street,
1880, Hippolyte J Blanc
Chunky stuff: generally French Gothic in style,
it consists of a wide barn with a very stony

Original perspective of the Regal

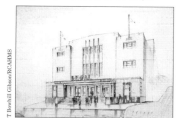

gable facing the street with rose window and stringcourse, dignified by a buttressed tower and octagonal stone spire against its south-western flank.

Hoban Square
Gigantic courtyard of single-storey hotel alms-houses with plentiful glazing and good entrances, unified by a heavy, deep timber fascia.

Fairfield Garage, *c*.1928, has a flat-headed art deco pediment. Adjacent **Bell's Whisky HQ**, 1958, by J & F Johnston & Partners, very

Bell's Whisky HQ

Jaques

good of its type; slight two-storey brick box with projecting first-floor oriel window. Everything is dominated by the **railway viaduct**, *c*.1840, John Miller, of the engineering firm of Granger & Miller, a competent architect (e.g. Haymarket Station in Edinburgh). Edinburgh & Glasgow railway was begun in 1838, and opened in 1842. This immense viaduct curving across the Almond flood plain consists of a wide principal arch flanked by three smaller arches, with abutment decorated with incised ornament in Miller style.

Railway viaduct

Eydmann

Kilpunt doocot
All the trappings of a 17th-century decorative doocot, two-storey cylindrical (now robbed of its harling) with semicircular upper storey windows. Uneasy conical roof (now felted).

85 Illieston, 1665
At the end of a tree-lined avenue, this dignified Scots house built for John Ellis of Elliston is two-and-a-half storey with dormer windows, crowstepped gable to the front, a projecting square tower of rooms to the back with a turnpike stair in the re-entrant. Buildings to

Top *Avon aqueduct*. Middle, right and above *Glimpses of the Scottish Middle Ages: Torphichen Preceptory*

Top *Cairnpapple*. Left *Detail, Gowanbank*. Above *Civic art, Bathgate: Princess Marjory visits the steelyard by Lynn Clarke*

Top *Easter Inch, by Bathgate.* Left *Bathgate Academy.*
Above *18th-century view of Balbardie House*

Morris & Steedman

A L Hunter Photography

Corrance/WLDC

Top *Mandela Bridge: the most modern bridge in this much be-bridged valley is probably the most beautiful.*
Above *Private house by Donald McInnes at Houstoun House.*
Left *Kirkhill*

Top *View over Central Scotland from Knock Hill.* Above *Beecraigs Reservoir.* Left *Strathbrock St Nicholas, Uphall*

Top *Elibank Children's Centre.*
Above *Original perspective of the
Cameron Ironworks.*
Top right *Stoneyburn Primary School*

Right *Finial surging from the
Sandilands' Burial Vault, St John's
Parish Church, Mid Calder.*
Below *Diagnostic Sonar, Kirkton
Campus, Livingston*

Two visions of Scotland: Top *The Five Sisters shale bing at Addiewell at their most romantic.* Above *The dying glories of pre-Reformation Scotland: St John's Parish Church, Mid Calder*

Top *Harburn House in its pastoral setting.* Above *Cullen enclosure, Kirknewton.* Above right *Easter Colzium and the rim of the Pentlands.* Right *Cobbinshaw Reservoir by Richard Jaques*

Illieston, as it would look if the harling were restored

Henry Erskine (1746-1817), a younger son of the 10th Earl of Buchan, was twice Lord Advocate for Scotland – in 1783 and 1806, Dean of the Faculty of Advocates from 1785, and Member of Parliament – first for Fife, and then for Haddington & Dumfries. Possibly the outstanding lawyer of his time, Lord Cockburn recorded: *In his profession, he was the very foremost. No rival approached him in the variety, extent or brilliancy of his general practice. Wherever there was a litigant, civil, criminal, fiscal or ecclesiastic, then there was a desire for Harry Erskine ... Nothing was so sour as not to be sweetened by the glance, the voice, the gaiety, the beauty of Harry Erskine ... He deserves our reverence for a delightful temper, safe vivacity and unmatched professional splendour.* He was known as the poor man's advocate.

one side of the forecourt, and a splendid split-pediment gate-pier. Shorn of harl, and in deep russet rubble, it is not entirely convincing as though Illieston – like Houstoun, Kirkhill and so many others – has undergone alteration. Unusual dormer windows, blocked windows/entrances in the west gable, and three blind armorial panels on the north façade, two of them forming a stack with the windows that would normally be above the main entrance.

86 Almondell & Calderwood Country Park

Lovely ravine of the River Almond and its feeders, the Murieston and Linhouse Waters, opened as a country park in the 1970s. The **Visitor Centre**, *c.*1790, coachhouse and stables for the curiously unsophisticated **Almondell House** (designed by its owner Henry Erskine in 1786 and demolished in 1969) is symmetrical with pedimented two-storey centre section flanked by pavilion-roofed wings and other offices. *Guidebook available.*

In front is the Earl of Buchan's **Astronomical Pillar**, 1776, removed from Kirkhill House; a square pier, incised with Latin inscriptions and astronomical equations, surmounted by a belltower and cross. Walks are peculiarly beautiful.

Almondell

Henry Erskine designed Almondell House himself and suffered the perils of an amateur architect. His son (12th Earl of Buchan) was unimpressed with the result. *He made his residence at Almondell consist of at least two houses connected by an inconvenient sort of gallery; the access to the best rooms was through a long narrow passage. He hollowed away all of the ground to make offices under the old house, so that it cracked all the way up one side. He made those under the new house dark and damp. The floor would not keep out the water, the foundation would not let it away. His ice house had a southern aspect. His coal cellars had trap doors under the front windows.*

Left *Almondell Stables.*
Below *Almondell House (demolished)*

Almondell and its bridges:
Top *Aqueduct.* Above *Aerial view of the viaduct.* Top right *Mandela Bridge.* Middle right *Nasmyth Bridge with its fanciful rustic detail.* Right *Camps Viaduct*

Opposite (from top to bottom) *Fauldhouse; villa in Crofthead; Crofthead Primary School; Longridge Church; Stoneyburn Church*

Nasmyth Bridge, *c.*1800, attributed to painter and architect Alexander Nasmyth (1759-1840), has two rustic arches of differing spans unified by a crenellated parapet. **Aqueduct**, 1820, by Hugh Baird, cast-iron trough cantilevered from stone abutments feeding the Union Canal. **Camps Viaduct** carried a branch of the North British Railway serving James Young's Paraffin Light & Mineral Oil Company at

Pumpherston on nine segmented brick arches. **Mandela Bridge**, Shielsmill, 1971, by Morris & Steedman with Tom Ridley, is a most elegant suspension footbridge composed of slender cables supported on a single pylon from which hangs a lightweight footbridge (colour page C12).

The **Union Canal Aqueduct**, *c.*1820, by Hugh Baird sweeps the canal round over the Almond in five great rubbly buttressed arches.

FAULDHOUSE

High moor-edge former mining community, with substantial ashlar cottages in **Main Street**. **St Andrew's Kirk**, Main Street, 1866, by Angus Kennedy, is buttressed Gothic with traceried window and elegant door. **St John the Baptist**, 1873, by W & R Ingram, is plainer – a simple broad-shouldered chapel with corbelled belfry and spirelet above a rose window with Star of David tracery. Stained glass by Hardman, E M Dinkel, 1856, and J Blyth, 1951-6. Substantial villas in Crofthead. The **Caledonia Hotel**, 1895, appropriately brash for a former station hotel, has oriel windows and a lofty pedimented door. What Fauldhouse requires is concentration – a town centre, with higher density for greater focus with a new role in upland recreation.

Many good cottages, most single-storey, in **Sheephousehill**, including a delightful one with a central pediment with trefoil window. **Crofthead Primary School**, *c.*1900, a huge, three-storey pile with crowstepped gables, stringcourses, roundels and finials, dominates.

Longridge

Highest village in West Lothian with spectacular 360° views. A long linear straggle on the route from Lanark to Linlithgow focused on the boxy Gothic-windowed **Church**, 1840, by Robert Black.

STONEYBURN

Unfettered by urban design, with a few sporadic monuments. Small cream-rendered **Church of Scotland** is unusually pretty; buttressed gable to the street with a heavy Arts & Crafts belfry. Nearby **Stoneyburn House** has a long pedigree proven by datestones of 1655, 1670, 1678, 1713 and 1759. **Stoneyburn Primary School**, 1986, Lothian Regional Council Architects, is a nucleus of

Right *Bents*. Above *Stoneyburn Primary School*

flat-roofed, brown-brick hexagons with horizontal glazing (colour page C14). **Bents**, 1919, is an early development of 138 homes in *a fit country for heroes to live in* built by United Collieries; likewise **Garden City**, built by the West Lothian Housing Society.

Loganlea House, 1798
Window irregularity and the raggle of a former projecting wing indicates something 17th-century. Fine rolled mouldings to door and window surrounds: south front wall-head has a chimney corbelled out above a Venetian window.

Top right *Addiewell Main Street, c.1900. This view has vanished.* Top *St Thomas RC Church.* Above *Faraday Place.* Right *Meadowhead House*

ADDIEWELL, from 1865
One of Paraffin Young's largest oil works. Shale oil communities characteristically took the form of long, low, single-storey, brick cottages, placed at random in unlikely rural locations – like **Faraday Place**, *c*.1890. Addiewell has no real centre, unless you count its crowstepped

farm, 1762. **St Thomas RC Church**, 1923, by Reginald Fairlie, sitting high and harled on its raised site, has a baroque gable with niche for a statue at the apex. **Priest's house** with pyramid roof adjoins. The most eye-catching feature of Addiewell is the Five Sisters shale bing, the most predominant surviving symbol of the oil industry. **Meadowhead House**, 1899, by J G Fairley, is an impressive three-storey baronial tower grafted upon an Improvement farmhouse.

[87] **Auchenhard House**, *c.*1800
Forceful upmarket farmhouse (once harled) with pavilion roof, central chimneystacks and good classical doorway. Ivy-clad ruin of its predecessor with elegant approach stair to its pedimented first-floor entrance lies nearby. **Auchenhard Tower**, by the Breich Burn in a lovely secluded meadow, may be the ruins of a folly or doocot.

WHITBURN
Polkemmet Country Park
Whitburn's economy is closely tied to that of Polkemmet, ancient seat of the Baillies, early agricultural improvers and philanthropists who founded Baillie Institutes in Whitburn, Blackburn, Fauldhouse, Longridge and Harthill (forerunners of community centres). Polkemmet (demolished) was a substantial house, the principal mansion block (originally 17th-century) later castellated in the David Hamilton manner. Extended baronially in Victorian times and, in 1912, by Dick Peddie & Forbes Smith. The heavily wooded 170-acre estate opened as a country park in 1971, facilities focused upon golfers. Stable block a **Visitors' Centre**.

Parish Church, Manse Road, 1729, slumbers peacefully on a bluff to the south; a plain cross-plan kirk with round-headed windows, bellcote and perch (lacking harl). **Laird's loft** within to the Baillies of Polkemmet. Fine monuments;

J G Fairley (1846-1934) lived and worked in Meadowhead House, West Calder, the baronial towered extension of which he built in 1899. An accomplished architect, he designed numerous fine buildings in West Lothian with sensitivity and competence; but in the building of St David's, Bathgate, and Linlithgow Academy he displayed great creative imagination. In Edinburgh he baronialised that well-known landmark, the 17th-century Kirkbrae House at the Dean Bridge (see *Edinburgh* in this series). Other designs include St Mary's RC Chapel, Ratho, 1880; Co-operative building, West Calder, 1884; Congregational Church, Bathgate, 1885; Parish Church, Balerno, 1888; St Nicholas Free Church, Broxburn, 1890; Free Church, Uphall, 1896; Braid School, Addiewell, 1896; Linlithgow Academy, 1900; Dreadnought Hotel, Bathgate, 1901; church at Blackridge, 1901; St David's, Bathgate, 1904; Balbardie Primary School, 1904; RC School, Addiewell, 1916.

Below Auchenhard Tower. Bottom Elevation, Polkemmet House (demolished)

Jaques

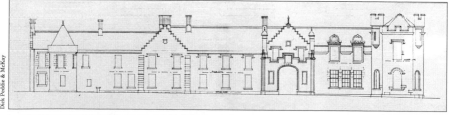

Dick Peddie & McKay

The cast-iron memorial, white-painted with black lettering, is to *Dear sweet Bess*, Elizabeth Burns, daughter of the poet and spouse of John Bishop at Polkemmet, who died on 8 Jan. 1817, aged 32, and her daughter, Mary Lyon, who died just over three months later aged just under two: and to John Bishop himself, the bereaved husband, who died almost exactly 40 years later aged 75.

Right *Burgh Hall*. Above *Elizabeth Burns' Memorial*

Polkemmet Pithead Baths, 1934 (demolished), had a striking symmetrical butterfly plan of locker rooms, canteen and bathhouse climaxing in gleaming white service tower with semicircular glazed stair; a real 1930s rocket-launcher of a building. The **colliery** was nicknamed the *Dardanelles* either because its opening coincided with that disastrous campaign or because of the number of lives lost in sinking its shafts and working its faces. Following the Miners' Strike of 1985, and consequent flooding of the pit, Polkemmet ceased operations, bringing to an end all coal mining in West Lothian.

Above *Gala Day in Whitburn*.
Right *Brucefield Church of Scotland*

the iron memorial to Elizabeth Burns, daughter of the poet, and the delightful stone to John Weir, mason.

The **Burgh Hall**, a smart *c.*1830 civic building with good ashlar, stringcourse and quoined pilasters, has been extended to the east, transformed by new windows and a giant baroque entrance, and diminished by a wall-head gable with its dinky, slate-hung, ogee-roofed clock-tower. To its west is a sturdy 1815 house with wall-head gables and dated scrolled skewputts. Isolated Victorian villas in **West Main Street**, interspersed with some sedate and well-built cottages – particularly **No 46 Ramsay Place**. The 1969 harled towers of **Millbank**, Gordon Duncan Somerville, have been given pitched stepped-back roofs. **Fire Station**, 1972, by Walker & Cunningham, sits like an overscaled harled cottage, with a deep fascia of the oversailing roof to its appliance shed like a chinaman's hat.

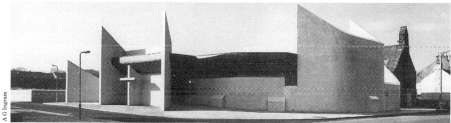

A G Ingram

Brucefield Church of Scotland, 1966,
Rowand Anderson Kininmonth & Paul
Fine ground-hugging kirk in the modern Scots
tradition on the corner of Brucefield Road,
enclosing a courtyard with the existing belfried
kirk: strong geometric roughcast walls support
its bellying roof. Swedish-influenced interior.

Brucefield Church of Scotland

Whitburn Academy, Shanks Road, 1967,
Wheeler & Sproson
Simplicity of the four-storey teaching block on
columns attracts attention, with its
interlocking storey-height, precast-concrete
panels, with ribbed spandrels.

In 1804, Whitburn was *an inland village, the residence of some shopkeepers, and a considerable number of tradesmen necessary to the accommodation of the country and the neighbourhood ... Many persons are employed as weavers by the Glasgow manufacturers. The village is not of ancient date, and has been formed chiefly in consequence of the cottages having been destroyed which were formerly scattered over the country, and the inhabitants having removed into villages. The parish was one of the earliest where enclosures ended Lowland crofting.*

Harvey Photography

Jaques

Above *Newhouse Roadhouse.*
Left *Whitburn Academy*

[88] **Newhouse Roadhouse**, *c.*1936
Aimed at the A8 car traveller; geometric,
white-harled corner windows. Streamlining
imagery lessened by tall steeply pitched roof
and current neo-Georgian glazing.

BLACKBURN
Former cotton community based around a
water-powered mill on the Almond, Blackburn
expanded as a coalmining town. Almost
entirely sandwiched between the A705 and the
M8 stretching out to Bathgate, its population
virtually doubled between 1960-70 with the
arrival of the BMC truck plant in Bathgate.
With its closure, it has slipped back again.
Church of Scotland, Main Street, 1908, by
Roberts & Paul, is village-scaled, harled with
some unconvincing Gothic detail. **Murrayfield**

Rural house contemporary mode by Richard Murphy at Stone Heap Farm, Stoneyburn

Murphy

Right *Golden Circle Hotel.*
Above *Church of Scotland*

Primary School, Catherine Terrace, 1965, by Alison & Hutchison & Partners, has crisp harling, inclined roofs with timber fascias and hard, black-edged windows. **Golden Circle Hotel**, *c.*1966, faced the truck plant brashly; white, edged with black, perched above an

arched colonnade, a tall black-and-white crowned spire as a landmark. Cheap flat-roofed groups of houses with cutaway corners on either side of Bathgate Road have been handsomely enveloped, harled and pitch-roofed by SSHA. Sustained pressure from a residents' group, architectural advisor Tom Henney, has transformed the crude 1960s concrete maisonette slab-and-point blocks of **Murrayfield** (thrown up in a hurry to accommodate workers for the truck plant) with curious Chinese touches, some slabs reduced to terraces.

Blackburn Town Centre, 1968,
Wheeler & Sproson
Brave New (multi-functional) World – bank, supermarket, library, hotel and flats flanking and straddling a bleak pedestrian mall of shops which lost its optimism as Blackburn has lost its economy. The mono-pitched roofed flats, starkly white-harled with black-edged windows, are the most geometric.

Blackburn Town Centre

Seafield
Excellent Scandinavian houses; with alternating mono-pitched roofs, slender chimneys and informal groupings creating both a sense of enclosure and style, *c.*1970.

89 **Blackburn House**, *c.*1765
Janus-faced house: ceremonial north front, with later Doric porch, presents pedimented and pavilion-roofed picture of gentility flanked by a screen to pavilions. But first-floor windows do not light generously proportioned rooms (the attic floor runs across their middle). East and

west it appears not as a country mansion but as a farmhouse; and those pavilions as barns. East/west passage beneath the house. Fine drawing and dining rooms with plaster ceilings and bay windows with a splendid view south. After 20 years of neglect, restoration pursued by Simpson & Brown for Blackburn House Building Preservation Trust.

Top Seafield. Above Elevation of Blackburn House

LIVINGSTON
Designated as a New Town in 1962, Livingston now has a population of over 43,000, making it the second largest urban area in Lothian and its greatest concentration of modern industry. Until Nissan was built, Livingston was host to the largest Japanese investment in Europe. The town's 10 square miles of rolling landscape rise up to Dechmont Law in the north and down to the lovely Almond Valley which acts as its spine. Other watercourses – the Murieston Water, Killandean Burn, and Folly Burn – around which so much of the town's splendid landscape, trails, greenways and bicycle routes have been created – drain into the Almond. Mansions, farms, mills and mines have been

Livingston: Below Landscape of the River Almond in the town centre. Bottom Sidlaw and Pentland Houses

85

Top *Almondvale sculpture area.*
Middle *Livingston Parish Kirk.*
Above *Folly Burn*

absorbed, providing the new with a heritage anchor unusual in such New Towns.

Its layout in groups of *environmental areas*, by which traffic is channelled around the perimeter, renders Livingston very private. You could drive through it with no other impression than desultory housing, or factories located within trees. The housing has developed from the 1960s medium-rise high density (as in Craigshill), to the 1970s preoccupation with the place of the car in housing areas (and the creation of an environment in which people dominate), to the lower density, low-rise suburban approach of the late 1980s and '90s.

The quality of industrial design and landscape has been central to the drive to attract new companies. The *advance factory* – speculative developments of varying levels of quality aimed at particular market sectors – has been developed to a sophisticated level. In Brucefield, for example, all buildings are of a rationalised design and construction system intended to achieve high-quality, flexible buildings with greater efficiency in the mid-range of advance factories. More recent advance factories are increasingly streamlined with curved corners in automotive imagery.

90 **Town Centre**
Focus of administration, shopping, offices and a statutory hotel, rather than a *high street* or *market place* (a town square is now under design), **Almondvale** occupies a plateau just south of the river, enfolded by distributor roads. Two, linear, six-storey, eye-catching slabs with white mosaic panels – **Pentland House**, 1979, and **Sidlaw House**, 1981, both designed by Michael Laird & Partners – sit at right angles, and sandwich the 1974 **Almondvale Centre**, by Hay Steel & MacFarlane. **Grampian Court** and **Lomond House** are horizontally proportioned with strongly emphasised brick buttresses, in either a dark-brown or a royal-red brick. **Bank of Scotland**, 1988, Forgan & Stewart, is a financial fortress; crisply detailed in grey panels and dark glazing.

91 **Livingston Village**
Livingston's origins lie at Livingston Peel whose foundations have been re-created at the end of a long and ingenious boardwalk by Folly Burn. The village retains much small-scale charm. **Manse**, 1803 (it looks later), is a

Livingston Inn

Livingston Place succeeded the tower of Livingston Peel: its name implying it was probably a courtyard mansion. It became the home of Sir Patrick Murray, an enthusiastic horticulturist. Following several visits to the continent in the early 18th century, he built up a unique collection of flowers and shrubs. Following his death, the collection was transferred eventually to become the basis of Edinburgh's Royal Botanic Garden.

handsome L-shaped block, entrance in the angle, likewise stripped of the harling implied by its window and corner margins. Pleasant cottages face the **Main Street**. Long white two-storey 18th-century row, **The Danders**, frames the village green. **Bloom House**, c.1850, good plain and stolid L-plan, has rounded corners and dormer windows. White-harled **Livingston Inn**, a former coaching inn on the Edinburgh/Glasgow turnpike, has a pantiled stable courtyard. The **Parish Kirk**, 1732, basks in the economic bosom of the enfolding New Town, a lovely building on an ancient site, surrounded by a splendid graveyard with lively headstones (notably that to Thomas Graham, 1769, of Seafield, with a central cartouche flanked by a sower and reaper). Octagonal chimneys at one end, louvred bird-cage belfry at the other. 1970s housing at **Millfield** and **Burnfield**, just to the west, was the first use of courts which mixed pedestrians and vehicles.

Below *Livingston Peel as drawn by Timothy Pont, 1592; The Oil Museum; Bloom House; Old Toll House as it may originally have looked. Left Livingston Mill Farm*

92 **Almond Valley Heritage Centre**, 1992, Comprehensive Design
The **Oil Museum**, a smart green high tech pavilion with curving glass walls, includes an exploration of the sensations and depth of a shale mine. In **Livingston Mill Farm**, 18th

and 19th centuries – attractive steading, house, cornmill and ancillary buildings, rubble, slated and pantiled – the 16ft-diameter undershot millwheel is now fully restored and in action. Idyllic scene with mill lade, river, courtyards and ducks.

93 **Old Toll House**, Long Livingston, c.1800
Broad-shouldered pedimented toll house, originally three square windows at first floor with carving in the centre of the pediment.

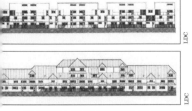

Top *Alderstone House.* Above *Alderstone doocot.* Right *Geometric vision of Craigshill as first built*

94 **Alderstone House**, largely early 17th century Old crowstepped Scots mansion, its west wing a decapitated early 16th-century tower (ground-floor vault, but turnpike stair removed); extended twice in the 17th century with more palatial apartments; then reception rooms on the ground floor and a two-storey bay added in the 19th. Fine crowstepped lectern **doocot**. **Steading** glazed over to form an airy garden court. Note the 1993 DC housing at **Eliburn**, off Alderstone Road.

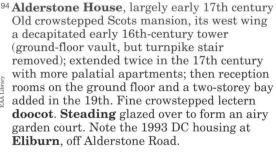

Craigshill exemplifies the spartan and geometric approach to the early New Town. The **Road Research Laboratory**, 1967, Architectural Research Unit, is a discrete and well-proportioned U-shaped block, glazing modulated by concrete ribs. Everything is dominated by the cheaply built **Jespersen blocks**, 1964, a pioneeringly odd idea to build family maisonettes above flats, each with its own glass-fronted terrace or balcony. Refurbishment with pitched roofs has diminished their geometry but gained urbanism. **Corston** and **Pentland Parks**, 1966, Philip Cocker & Partners, represent good high-density, low-rise homes with Scandinavian mono-pitch roofs.

Top *Jespersen blocks as originally designed.* Middle *As now converted.* Above *Almond South housing*

95 **Shiel Walk**, 1988, Development Corporation Architects Post-modern refurbishment of heavy blocks with variously coloured, rendered panels, each with tiled portico, vague Ionic capitals to the columns, keyhole pediment above. **Fire Station**, 1967, by Bamber & Hall, perhaps the best building in Craigshill, its ribbed-concrete hose tower with its black cantilevered balconies being one of Livingston's landmarks.

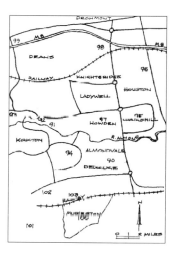

St Andrew's RC Church

St Andrew's RC Church, 1968, GRM Kennedy & Partners, is a dramatically convoluted swirl of shutter-marked concrete high on the hillside.

Houston Industrial Estate, to the north, is dominated by the sober, rectangular, metal-clad tower of **Abbey Chemicals**, and the vast **Cameron Iron Works**, 1963, by Matthews Ryan & Partners (colour page C14).

⁹⁶ **Pumpherston**
Built to house workers from the highly profitable oil refinery, those who could, stayed somewhere better like Mid Calder. The rest remained in miners' rows (originally brick, now harled) running at right angles from the road. The contrast between the condition of Pumpherston and that of Livingston New Town, barely yards to the west, is truly awesome. West Calder Co-operative, the only three-storey building in Pumpherston, occupies a corner site, its former windows boarded, its stumpy clock-tower defying decay.

LIVINGSTON: North

Howden House

⁹⁷ **Howden House**, *c.*1770
Lying at the top of the brow overlooking the 33 acres of parkland, this lovely, harled, substantial mansion with flanking wings, margined windows, enormous chimneystacks

Above *Howden stable block extension*. Right *Eliburn Children's Centre*. Below *Inveralmond Community High School*. Bottom *Knightsridge Nursery School*

and a Doric porch, is now in use as a community centre. The **stable block** now forms the **Howden Park Centre**; extended with hall, theatre, studios and dining room, 1970, by L'D C Architects.

Roman Catholic High School, Braehead roundabout, 1994, Lothian Regional Council Architects
Clever double-spine plan like a college around internal streets determinedly post-modern in its patterned walls and jagged profile.

Children's Centre, Eliburn, 1988, Lothian Regional Council Architects
A gingerbread house: a Hansel & Gretel building in light brick with red banding, with a wealth of interesting detail, including a carefully modelled and textured roof in tile and slates (colour page C14). **Adult Training Centre**, 1982, Lothian Regional Council Architects, is an enormous cottage pavilion, sharp red brick, buttresses and oversailing tiled roof. **Inveralmond Community High School**, 1977, Lothian Regional Council Architects, is elegant and crisp with concrete panels on a brick plinth, its long horizontality punctuated by its stair-towers and octagonal brick outshots containing halls.

98 **Knightsridge House**, 1831
Two-storey classical cube on an ancient site up Dechmont Law, named after the Knights Hospitallers of St John of Torphichen. Unusual pedimented Ionic portico facing north and extraordinary massing of its chimneys to the centre of its pavilion roof. Converted into flats and extended.

Margaret Blackwood housing, Nether Dechmont, 1983, Penton & Appleton

Quadrangle of white pitched-roof cottages modulated by outsized timber-framed porticos, flower boxes ingeniously suspended from the eaves. **Knightsridge Nursery School**, 1976, West Lothian District Council Architects, small scale with projecting curved towers in white roughcast with sliced-off roofs.

Deans was centred on the old shale-oil village of Livingston Station: but there are no longer any bings, and the station is now a mile east by Carmondean. Note particularly the **church**, 1949, Ian G Lindsay, typically Scots harled and slated with a pyramid-roof tower. **School**, 1906, (now youth centre) has art nouveau details at the entrances. **St Paul's Church**, Carmondean, 1980, by F R Stephenson, rides the contours with a series of jagged harled gables and pantiled mono-pitched roofs providing clerestory lighting into the kirk. The octagonal **Copper Tun** pub, 1981, Waters Jamieson Partnership, has gently pitched metal roofs and a tourie top-knot.

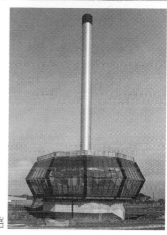

[99] **MOTEC**, Deans Industrial Estate, 1970, Newman Levinson & Partners
Only Livingston landmark known to M8 drivers (as they drive round the woody posterior of Dechmont Law through the Deans Industrial Estate) is the circular see-through boiler house of the **Multi-Occupational Training & Educational Centre** and its adjacent heavy goods vehicle building. Even more striking is the adjacent **Schlumberger Training School**, SGA Buildings, 1974, with its three poised drilling rigs and lightweight semi-circular canopies. On the north side of the

Top *Margaret Blackwood housing.*
Above *MOTEC boiler house.*
Left *NEC*

motorway resides the spreading empire of **NEC** in its gleaming white skin and dark glazing, 1982, Michael Laird & Partners. The large, 1987, full wafer-production factory, by the Parr Partnership, is a three-storey sandwich; a clean room between air handling above and extraction below.

Kirkton Campus
The quality of Scotland's first high-technology park can best be appreciated as you sweep

Livingston industry: Top *Canon Business Machines.* Above *Advance factory.* Right from top *Ethicon; Seagate Micro Electronics; W L Gore; Shin-Etsu*

downhill along Simpson Parkway. Three hundred acres of landscaped luxuriance on either side of the Killandean Burn spread out before you, coruscating with gleaming, crisp or smooth-edged pavilions. **Ethicon**, 1978, by Michael Laird & Partners occupies one-seventh of the entire campus; white linear boxes with a thin strip window for the production building, brown brick and large glazing for the administration block. **W L Gore**, 1984, was designed by Michael Laird & Partners to encourage interaction between research and development within a cohesive production unit of 250 staff. Triangular in plan, the administration building acts as outer skin for the darker production building which it enfolds. **Logic**, 1994, Carl Fisher Sibbald, is a clever, square, cream-and-blue pavilion, a corner cut away and replaced by a round entrance and protruding rectangular tower. The health care factory **Boehringer Mannheim**, 1982, Livingston Development Corporation Architects, comprises single-storey administration building in horizontal brick with rhythmic buttresses, and two-storey office block, the precise brickwork shielding the aluminium-clad manufacturing facility behind. **Canon Business Machines**, 1989, by the Parr Partnership, opts for a floating pavilion, principal floor cantilevered out beyond the entrance floor, all tied together by an oversailing pitched roof supported on columns. **Seagate Micro Electronics**, 1986, Livingston Development Corporation Architects, requires air cleanliness a thousand times greater than a hospital operating theatre, and so all machinery likely to transmit vibration is on separate foundations. Separate crisp blue cubes, horizontal glazing contrast with solid service stacks and opaque panels to the production area.

DEDRIDGE

The ecumenical **Lanthorn Community complex**, Kenilworth Rise, 1976, by G R M Kennedy & Partners, is a harled, flat-roofed and horizontally proportioned ziggurat. **James Young High School**, 1981, by Lothian Regional Council Architects resembles an enormous cottage hospital: giant sweeping roofs and breakwalls enfold pleasantly stepped landscape areas. Some early harled houses have been enlivened by the town artist.

Top *Logic*. Above *Lanthorn Community complex*. Left *Bankton House*

Bankton House Hotel, 1812, Charles Black
Delightful Regency villa built originally for James Bruce, Secretary for Excise for Scotland. Plainly elegant, with its single-storey wings, it is distinguished by the splendid ground-floor windows within their arcaded recesses, fanlit door and Doric porch.

Murieston House

100 **Murieston House**, *c.*1830
Upstream, classical mansion built for John Learmonth of Murieston with a central

Murieston Castle

pedimented projecting entrance bay, the door sandwiched by twin pilasters. **Murieston Castle**, a tiny roofless ruin in the farm policies, was probably converted to a folly in the early 19th century. The corbelling of the turret is too accurate and too lavish to be altogether fake, despite the 1815 heraldic device sitting over twin 1825 Gothic arches.

101 **Westfield House**, 1760
More Irish than Scottish: delightful, unusual house of plain, five-bay, two-storey central block with harl, dressed margins and enormous chimneystacks flanked by projecting wings with stringcourses acting as pediments and round-headed windows within. Chimneys are panelled.

102 **Bellsquarry**
Bells Quarry was the source of stone for Edinburgh's National Monument on Calton Hill (see *Edinburgh* in this series). The village is now a peaceful oasis. Pleasant **Elm Tree Inn** – two-storey, rubble, part of a row, with Doric pilasters. **Brucefield Farm** is a handsome, substantial Improvement farmhouse, *c*.1800 – three-bay, elegant door, flanking wings – rescued by the District Council; now a restaurant. **Smiths & Ritchie**, by Livingston Development Corporation, is a crisp, well-proportioned, silver-clad printing works in Brucefield Park West.

103 **Newpark**, 1806
Diminutive villa with projecting flat-headed pedimented entrance bay somewhat overwhelmed by a bay-windowed extension to the east, and bay windows added to the original block.

Below *Westfield House in the late 19th century*. Bottom *Brucefield Farm*. Right *Newpark*

WEST CALDER

WLDC Libraries

13-19 Main Street

The commercial centre of 19th-century oil-boom Scotland lining the ridge above the West Calder Burn: much changed since the **Old Parish Church**, 1643 (now a roofless ivy-clad rectangular ruin with square belfry, topped by a finial), celebrated the parish's freedom from Mid Calder. Slumbering gently amidst chestnut trees in a peaceful enclave off Kirkgate, it has handsome inscribed stones in the kirkyard – to John Jackson, merchant, 1786, and the urned monument to John Mowbray of Hartwood, 1852. **West Kirk**, c.1860, has a tall steeple with broach spire.

Town Centre

Of the three public monuments that used to identify the centre, **13-19 Main Street**, 1913, William Baillie, is the only survivor: pretty, smart (despite its current ghastly fascia) Co-operative building, tall three-storey patterned-stone emporium, openwork iron crown flanked by two crowstepped gables from which project bay windows. Replaced by the Royal Bank, the **People's Palace**, c.1885, by J G Fairley, was a

Below *Union Square and the former Co-op building*. Bottom *Drawing of the People's Palace from a Christmas card*. Left *West Calder Main Street*

Jaques

Jaques

Edinburgh Evening News

Top *Gowanlea House.* Above
Commercial Inn, Main Street

tall spiky confection like a fixed fairground comprising clock-tower, thistle tower and viewing gallery. Another Co-operative building, 1884, by J G Fairley, was demolished to make way for **Union Square**. A pedimented clock stands proud in one corner with a bronze plaque in memory of the 15 men who died in the Burngrange disaster in January 1947.

Co-operative Bakery, Society Place, 1910
Brick office block with flat-arched windowheads and curious corner turrets, lofty bakery (white-tiled internally) and stable yard, converted to West Calder Workspace, 1987, by Alan Tuffs and W L D C Architects. Two good octagonal corners frame **Gloag Place**: the Railway Inn's peaked, J McQue's ogee.

Gowanlea House, Stewart Street, *c.*1968
Large, three-storey, harled, L-shaped old people's home enclosing the attractive **King's Square**. Good modelling of simple elements; harled gables as pediments, expressed stair-tower with curved walls and irregular windows, and curved cornered balcony recesses.

Royal Bank of Scotland, 1978
Sweeping glazed drum flanked by brown-harled shoulders, the roof sliced off so cleanly as to give an architectonic meaning to the term *drum*.

Public Library, 1903, William Baillie
A jewel of a Carnegie library set high on the gushet with Harburn Road. Symmetrically designed, with art nouveau detailing around the entrance and pedimented Venetian windows to each side. Delightful two-storey interior with original tiling and glass.

Public Library from the west

65 Harburn Road, 1914, Edward Gatney
A very smart Arts & Crafts house by a
Newcastle architect; long low sweeping roof,
horizontal windows, beautifully proportioned
and detailed, with chunky timbers to porches
and front door frame. Jolly vine cornices and
Chinese balustrading to the stair within.

In **Polbeth** note the rows of dark-timbered and
elegant SSHA housing, 1938, by David Carr,
with white timber porches and lozenge
windows.

Top *65 Harburn Road.* Middle *West
Calder Station.* Above *1938
elevation of timber cottages in
Polbeth.* Left *Hermand House*

104 Hermand House, 1797
Splendidly austere classical mansion entered up
a raised perron to a gigantic pedimented
doorway with side windows. Gutted by fire in
the 1970s, it was restored as flats after
persistence by the District Council. **Coach
house** and **stables**, early 19th century, now
converted to a house, are rubble with central
pedimented section over a segmental archway.
The richly wooded policies created by Fergusson
from the dreary countryside of Hermandshiels
are a tribute to his passion for cultivation.

Limefield House, Polbeth, 1804
Smart five-bay villa in polished ashlar, the
central three bays slightly projecting and
capped by a pediment with oculus. Fine Doric
porch with splendid fanlight reached up a
flight of steps. Limefield became the home of

The builder of Hermand
House, George Fergusson, Lord
Hermand was one of Cockburn's
cronies: *Set upon George
Fergusson, at his paradise of
Hermand, during vacation, on
going forth for a long day's work
– often manual – at his farm
with a grey felt hat and tall
weeding hoe – what could be
more agrestic or picturesque …
What was it that made
Hermand such an established
wonder and delight? It seems to
me to have been the supremacy
in his composition of intensity of
temperament … He could not be
indifferent. Repose, except in
bed, was unnatural and
contemptible to him.* It was
Hermand, Cockburn recalled,
who, when sentencing a man to
death for murder when drunk
stated: *Good God, my Laards, if
he will do this when he is drunk,
what will he not do when he is
sober?*

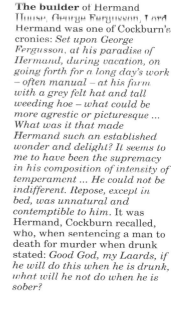

Limefield House

The Calders

In the 12th century, there was a small region known as Calatria, immediately west of Lothian: possibly the Calders. A heavily wooded area, Calder Wood being notable, it gave rise in later years to the following rhyme:

Cauther Wood was fair to see
(Calder)
When it went up to Camel tree
(Camelty)
Cauther Wood was fairer still
When it went up to Corset Hill
(Crosswoodhill)

Mid Calder was hardly dry: *There are nine public houses or dram shops. Every householder is at liberty to sell porter and ale during the fair. So many individuals being interested in the sale and consumption of ale and spirits has, no doubt, a most pernicious influence on the morals and habits of the inferior classes of the community, and has frequently been productive of consequences the most deplorable and distressing ... Being in the line of the great thoroughfare between Edinburgh and the populous towns of Glasgow, Ayr, Hamilton and Lanark, a vast number of idle, disorderly characters meet here and commit depradations and, as the public houses and dram shops are numerous, they frequently get intoxicated and disturb the peace of society.*
John Sommers, 1838

Mid Calder tolbooth was begun in August 1713 by the Bathgate mason George Waddell. Although called a prison house, it was very much more than that. The ground floor had four ashlar arcades sitting on stone pillars, this floor being terminated by a cornice. The *piano nobile* was harled, with three large windows lighting the Council Chamber. There were two cells on the ground floor, set nine feet back behind the arcades, the space in front designed as a covered market place. An external stair led up to a platform and into the Council Chamber. It was roofed in Stobo slate, supervised by Andrew Paterson, required to be built in nine months, and cost 1200 merks.

Paraffin Young. Dr David Livingstone stayed there during a visit back to Scotland in 1864 when he opened Young's Addiewell Works, and built a model of an African kraal.

MID CALDER

Set amidst the remnant of the once great Calder Wood, and strategically sited on the pendicle of land between the deep glens of the River Almond and the Linhouse Water, this little-known village was once a place of consequence – an important staging post on the 1763 turnpike road between Edinburgh and Glasgow via Whitburn, and on the cattle droving route between Falkirk and England (the beasts being driven through Cauldstane Slap in the Pentlands). Its prosperity was assured by three large mills on the Almond, the Oakbank shale works and the oily success of nearby Pumpherston.

Calder House, principally from 16th century Seat of the Sandilands, later Lords Torphichen, since 1350. The 1590s drawing of it by Timothy Pont implies one of the great Renaissance houses of Scotland; an enormously long slab with a fanciful skyline of chimneys, towers and cupolas. A tower, with thicker walls, is embedded at the heel of the house behind the two-storey semicircular entrance. The east wing is typically mid-16th-century in plan. In the early 17th century, the north wing was extended by a new stair-tower, with scale-and-platt stair up to the principal floors, a turnpike, corbelled out on its west side, up to a balustraded rooftop viewing platform. In the later 17th century, the north wing was extended again, in the style of Alexander McGill, immuring that balustraded platform at roof level, ending in a handsome four-storey quoined gable with round oculi. A comparable gable added to the south east. In c.1820, a circular two-storey Doric-porched entrance was added in the principal angle like the splayed entrance to Glamis and to Minto House. The former hall, now drawing room, retains its large Renaissance windows and fine panelling.

This was a demesne of grandeur: here John Knox may have celebrated his first Reformed Communion in Scotland in 1556; here Frédéric Chopin stayed. By stripping off its harl, flattening the roof and slicing off its dormer windows, history has conspired to diminish a great palace into a country mansion.

Calder House: Top left In 1894. Top In 1590 after Timothy Pont. Left The west façade showing the corbelled stair up to the balustraded roof viewing platform. Above Gates to Main Street

Many fine estate buildings: the splendid 1670 **gateway**, facing West Calder Road; a sharply broken pediment with ball finials, scrolls and alternate courses heavily rusticated; rustic **West Lodge**, pavilion roof, framed by tall chimneystacks and three identically scaled round-headed openings (lacking limewash); 17th-century **sundial**; round-shouldered **South Lodge** (hungrily rubble-pointed without its harl) and prettily bargeboarded **gate lodge** in Bank Street.

Steading, 1808, single-storey, entered beneath three-storey pedimented doocot. Large stable block partially restored by William A Cadell Architects.

Calder House Steading

Sandilands' 1540 specification for Mid Calder kirk included the following: *In the foresaid west gable ... a steeple to be raised thereupon 8ft broad and long, or 6ft broad and 12ft long, within the side walls of the said steeple, which side walls shall be of 6ft of height above the choir roof at all parts, with lights (openings) at all parts for the sound of the bells in the said steeple to be pierced, with a clock hand and bell in the place most suitable and convenient thereto ... And in the north angle, between the foresaid wall under the great arch and north wall of the kirk side, to raise a commodious (turnpike stair) to serve the rood loft of the said kirk and steeple foresaid, as easily as it may be had.*

St John's Parish Kirk: Above right *View from the east.* Right *In 1838.* Below *In c.1830, drawn by William Penny.* Bottom *Plan and elevation as originally intended, prepared by George Hay*

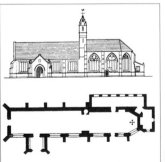

St John's Parish Church, Main Street, from 1541

Stunning evidence of the 16th-century ambitions of the Sandilands. Commissioned, designed and paid for by Magister Peter Sandilands who, as the younger son of the sixth Knight of Calder, went into the church to become rector of Mid Calder. The long seven-bay church, three in the choir and four in the nave (with a lower roof and rectangular windows) with cloister opening from the choir, had progressed beyond the vestry and foundations of the choir on Sandilands' death. He left minute instructions to his nephew, Sir James Sandilands of Calder, future Lord Torphichen, as to what was to be built. The nave was never begun. In 1863, Brown & Wardrop added the transepts and belfry (replacing the site of the village school). Pleasant 1595 wooden bench pew with the initials JS and IL inscribed *The Lord is my shepherd I shall not want*; with a tympanum of thistles. Stained glass, 1895, by Hardman in an 1883 memorial window to James Paraffin Young. Outstandingly rich carved finials rising from the sacristy. Conservation work by Stewart Tod & Partners (taking care to protect the bat colonies) (colour pages C14 & C15).

Brewery House, 70 Main Street, 18th century
Substantial house and south-facing garden,
gable and high stone wall to the street. Signs of
an older building within a c.1800 appearance
(e.g. square fanlight). Moulded cornice and
scrolled skewputts.

Main Street

Variously Church Street or High Street, linking
tolbooth, ancient market place and kirk. Decayed
in the 18th century, mostly rebuilt in the 19th
with sturdy artisan dwellings through shale-oil
money. **Property Shop** offers a confident curved
ashlar corner into the street. Its neighbour is a
substantial late 18th-century three-bay villa
with a moulded doorway. Next door, a former
pend has been filled in to form a gracious curved
window. 1890 tenements, what any self-
respecting industrial community thought it
ought to build, surge up incongruously. Further
south, there are whitewashed cottages, harled
houses and some elegant ashlar houses on the
west side with octagonal chimneyposts and
graceful doorways flanked with Doric columns.
No 71, 1894, a confident reworking of an older
building, has an ashlar façade and pantiled roof,
a fine window with hood-mould at ground floor,
swaggering first-floor gabled window with
pediment and datestone and, above all, art glass
in the square fanlight.

*Top 71 Main Street: note the fanlight
above the door. Above Brewery
House*

Bank Street

Good late 18th-century street architecture
against the leafy backdrop of **Calder Wood**.
Developed after the arrival of the
Edinburgh/Glasgow turnpike in 1763, Bank
Street has become Mid Calder's premier space;
particularly attractive in the way the road exits
at an angle at both ends making the space

Main Point, Bank Street

From the top: *Torphichen Arms*;
Clydesdale Bank; *17 Bank Street*;
39 Bank Street. Right *House facing
Bridge Street*

appear closed. The **Torphichen Arms**, *c.*1763, is the customary inn built by the laird. White-painted hostelry with scrolled skewputts, a later bay window and a handsome door.

Main Point
The fine harled curving bow terminating a row of substantial houses is the cynosure of Bank Street. Restored from a shell in 1987, it has distinguished triple window above a handsome stone-margined door. Pretty ashlar cottage with fine bracketed doorway alongside. These houses are Janus-faced; north frontage different from south. This row, once **Bridgend**, originally lay south of the main road to Edinburgh, until the handsome **South** (now **East) Bridge** was constructed in 1794 with its oculus (round hole) in the middle. The walk up **School Lane** leads past the

schoolhouse out to the Cunnigar (or Kinnungar), a curious tree-covered tumulus which offers lovely views of the countryside to the north.

The north side of Bank Street is the finest row of houses in Mid Calder; two-storey, late 18th-century, some harled, some limewashed and some rubble. The **Pend**, 1982, is a courtyard of harled town houses through a pedimented pend.

17 Bank Street, *c.*1860
Swaggering ashlar façade in the style of the British Linen Bank; corner pilasters with scrolls terminating the cornice, stringcourse, edged window surrounds, and cornices to main entrance and windows. Adjacent **Clydesdale Bank**, No 15, is ashlar, with quoins and tall

chimneystack, possibly by the same designer as **South Lodge** of Calder House.

Market Street
What a difference it would make if cobbled over again. Older houses at the east end, *c*.1804, large well-built square blocks, with later windows and doors. **Black Bull**, *c*.1860, a storey taller. **Post Office**, with later first-floor oriel windows, has nice stonework and quoins.

Calder Bank, Pumpherston Road, 1775
Elegant plain classical house, harled, with stone margins and moulded door.
Almondvale, Bridgend, late 18th century, three-bay like Calder Bank, is more vertical.

EAST CALDER
The largest of the Calders, predominantly a long main street stretching from the parish kirk to the gates of Almondell. **St Cuthbert's** is an ivy-clad, roofless, 16th century, rectangular ruin, belfry at the west, two lancet windows in the east, divided into burial enclosures for the Hares of Calder Hall and Blairlogie, and the Wilkies of Ormiston. Delightful 17th- and 18th-century gravestones of singular crudity.

Calder Hall, *c*.1824 (demolished), ?Robert Reid
Sophisticated Greek Revival mansion; marginally projecting wings, windows recessed within panels, Ionic pilasters at the set-backs beckoning to stupendous Ionic-columned and pilastered porch and doorway.

Merivale Cottage, 258 Main Street, *c*.1824
Ashlar cottage with the atmosphere of a dower-house. Doric-columned doorway, projecting quoins and flanking pavilions to each side.

From the top: *Market Street; Calder Bank; Column detail of Calder Hall; Calder Hall (demolished).* Left *Merivale Cottage*

Above *Parish Church & Public Library*. Right *East Calder Health Centre*

Parish Church, 1888
Smart Gothic gable facing the street with landmark clock-tower and spire adjacent. **Public Library**, 1987, by West Lothian District Council Architects, has low deep-eaved pavilion roofs, blockwork walls and cut-away windows. Further along the street is a row of terraced cottages, 1924, with cat-slide overhanging windows, built by the Scottish Veterans Garden City Association. The **square**, off the other side of Main Street, of houses, shops and flats is remarkably anachronistic for 1970, when it was built by Midlothian County Council Architects.

East Calder Health Centre, 1982,
Nicholas Groves-Raines
L-plan cathedral to health in agricultural barn aesthetic; harled, blue-metal roofed, nave lit by clerestory, huge gabled portholes at the corner and at the apex of the south transept. Slender cloister walk to the west: and entered through a leafy pergola to the east.

105 **Ormiston**, 1851, David Bryce
Busy crowstepped-gabled, turreted and dormer-windowed exterior, with square battlemented tower, conceals a relaxed mid-19th-century Victorian country-house plan, of which Bryce was the master. Fishscale slates on the turrets; service court to the east. It replaced the ruinous 17th-century **Ormiston**

Ormiston

Hill House, steep-roofed, three-bay, crowstepped laird's house with fine pedimented and pilastered doorcase.

Above *Ormiston Hill House.*
Left *Kirknewton Main Street*

KIRKNEWTON

More enclosed than many West Lothian villages: **Main Street** is narrow and winding, with a mixture of single- and two-storey cottages of mainly 19th century. **Dunallan**, 1840, has a curious mixture of a Georgian door framed by Tudor hood-moulds. **Kirkyard**, on its rolling sloping site, has the 1662 burial enclosure to the Campbell Maconachies of Meadowbank (now

Cockburn wrote: *Robert Cullen was a gentleman-like person in his manner, and learned in his profession, in which, however, he was too indolent and irregular to attain steady practice ... He had the misfortune to possess one power that seemed to exclude the exercise of all others. He was a mimic; and one of the very highest order.*

Left *Kirknewton kirkyard.* Below *Gravestone to James Smith, smith.* Bottom *Cullen burial enclosure*

Kirknewton House): another, dignified by an elaborate baroque broken-pedimented door, is to the Cullens; William Cullen (d.1790) – celebrated physician, botanist and philosopher – and Lord (Robert) Cullen (d.1810) – *eminent judge, elegant scholar and accomplished gentleman* (colour page C16). Some delightful 18th-century headstones – including that to James Smith, smith of Kirknewton, bearing his awl, adze and vice.

Parish Church, East Calder Road, 1750 Improvement kirk to serve East Calder and Kirknewton. Gothicised, 1872, by Brown & Wardrop, with Gothic south façade and adjacent saddle-back tower in fine ashlar with stringcourses. Delightful 1750 **manse**, (despite being stripped of its harl) elegant two-storey T-plan, central projecting gabled wing, with quoined door, windows and corners. **Highfield**, *c.*1840, opposite, is a handsome, much-chimneyed, Tudorish villa with bay windows and inset porch.

Right *Parish Church*. Below and bottom *Entrance lodge to Kirknewton House*. Below right *Kirknewton House*

Kirknewton House, from 17th century Ancient T-plan mansion, stripped down to rubble with Scots baronial additions, *c.*1835, by Playfair for Lord Meadowbank (when he

was creating Bonaly Tower for Lord Cockburn, and baronialising Craigcrook for Lord Jeffrey). Good balustraded screen wall to offices to the north. The **lodge** (now Huntingtower Inn), probably also by

Playfair, takes the form of a square tower with square ashlar turrets, tall dormer-windowed gallery-wing adjacent.

Hillhouse, *c*.1760
Handsome two-storey laird's house, Venetian window penetrating the cornice into a wall-head chimney. Nearby Gothic **Waterloo Tower**, 1815, was built as a folly to celebrate the battle: three-light lancet windows and crenellated, corbelled battlement. Would make an excellent tea-house.

106 **Hatton House**, 1692 (demolished, 1955)
One of the great Renaissance houses of Scotland, expanded from an original tower and later Renaissance courtyard by Lord Charles Maitland. It became a great rectangular mansion, circular towers on each corner, with an enormous balustraded viewing platform at the centre. Its surrounding policies were equally imposing – parterres, formal gardens and wilderness – some traces of which – including the ogee-roofed pavilions at each end – remain. Most splendid survival is the magnificent winged **gates**.

Mid Calder (Kirknewton) Station, *c*.1870
Wildly baronial with unreal crowsteps, crowstepped dormer windows, spiky chimneys – everything appropriate for a railway fantasy.

PENTLANDS
Lang Whang
The A70, far too prosaic a name for this lordly and lonely road, runs straight as a die from Carnwath to Colinton, with only peewit and curlew as company, and is the focus for scattered mansions and farmsteads in the beautiful southern uplands – for which **The Calders** delineate the northern, industrial boundary.

Top Hillhouse, Kirknewton. *Middle* Waterloo Tower. *Above* Gateway to Hatton House. *Left* Hatton House *drawn by Captain John Slezer, c.1680*

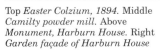

Top Easter Colzium, 1894. Middle Camilty powder mill. Above Monument, Harburn House. Right Garden façade of Harburn House

Easter Colzium, ?17th century
Remote, white, crowstepped, sturdily elegant, laird's house with square stair-tower and courtyard behind (colour page C16).

Camilty
Down in a wooded bend of Camilty Water, impressive ruin of the eight-bay, 19th-century **powder mill**, 2ft-thick crosswalls remaining like a deserted cathedral, and haunting policies of vanished Camilty. **Weir** and **falls** to the south.

107 **Harburn House**, 1804
Pretty two-storey Regency villa facing a courtyard; pavilion roof, dentilled cornice and curiously recessed central three bays with fine fanlit doorway. Three much more florid storeys facing north-west over an ornamental lake and beautifully landscaped policies. Now conference centre and hotel (colour page C16). A late 19th-century summerhouse faces the front

entrance. The early 19th-century **stables** form a plain elegant courtyard beneath the pedimented entrance. **Monument**, 1835, an ashlar Doric column topped by a ball finial, commemorates the visit of Charles X of France in 1832.

108 **Hartwood House**, from 1807 (*left*)
Large Improvement farmhouse, incorporating an earlier structure, transmogrified in harl and ashlar, *c*.1850, crowstepped bays squeezing a pedimented centre. Rebuilt after a fire to original façade by William A Cadell Architects.

109 **Broadshaw**, ?early 18th century (*left*)
Elegant, steep-roofed, white-harled, black-margined laird's house with later two-storey ashlar bay. The steading behind comprising barns and horsemill converted, 1985, by Alan Tuffs, into his own house.

Top *Harwood farmhouse*. Above
North façade of Linhouse in 1894.
Left *Linhouse from across the water*

110 Linhouse, 1589

Lovely crowstepped mansion on the north bank
of Linhouse Water extended in early 17th
century to U-plan. Normal entrance on the
north façade into the western wing. Principal
rooms on the first floor. Corbelled turrets.
Delightful and ornately corbelled turnpike stair
leading up to the rooftop viewing platform.
Principal stair to the first floor, corbelled
private stair in north-west corner to the upper
floors. Eastern tower contains spacious scale-
and-platt stair. Roof flatter than original,
dormers and harling gone. Fine panelling and
original moulded fireplaces within. Early 18th-
century **doocot**, oblong, crowstepped with two
elliptical openings above the doors. Profiting by
the fall in the Linhouse Water, a lake was
excavated in 1975. The **viaduct**, 1848, by
Joseph Locke, a six-span masonry structure,
carries the Caledonian Railway from Carstairs
to Edinburgh over the beautiful gorge.

111 Wester Causewayend, 1802

Fashionable reworking of something with a
long pedigree into an Improvement farmhouse
facing the Lang Whang. Slender proportions,

Joseph Locke (1805-60) was one of
Britain's leading railway engineers.
Born near Sheffield, he was
apprenticed to Stephenson, but soon
established himself on his own
track. Because he eschewed major
engineering works, his lines were
cheaper to build, but tended to be
more circuitous in route, more
steeply graded and more expensive
to operate. The Caledonian Railway,
begun in 1845, was a northwards
continuation of Locke's line from
Lancaster to Carlisle. Despite the
steep incline of Beattock, the line
was a great commercial success,
later extended to Perth and then
Dundee. It shared with the North
British the distinction of being the
busiest railway in Scotland.

slight asymmetry, older masonry and datestones indicate a site dating back to at least the 17th century. Doorway lintel inscribed John Graham Christine Sommervel, 1739. Built of handsome squared rubble (like whin), strong dentilled cornice, entrance deeply recessed within its corniced and architraved doorway.

112 **Old Schoolhouse**, Causewayend, 1823, James Gillespie Graham
Cairns Castle Coaching Inn, then a schoolhouse for forty years from 1875, now a house, reconstructed, from 1972, by Brian Edwards. Elegant single-storey long cottage with pavilion roof, centre three bays projecting. **Stables**, 1823, also by Graham, U-plan rubble courtyard (now houses) with ashlar dressings, screen walls and central gate-piers.

Right *Old Schoolhouse.*
Below *Remains of Cairns Castle*

Brian Edwards

EAA Library

113 **Cairns Castle**, from 1440
Seat of the Crichtons of Cairns, picturesquely sited on a knoll projecting into Harperrig Reservoir. Originally L-plan; a major and a minor tower with a turnpike staircase in the mutual corner. Customary cellars on the

ground floor, the kitchen fireplace later turned into a principal door. Entrance tower to the east now vanished.

114 **Ainville**, late 18th century
Handsome three-bay two-storey farmhouse with single-storey pavilion-roofed wings.

Ainville from the Lang Whang

115 **Templelands**, 1987,
William A Cadell Architects
Crisp, white-harled, grey-slated, T-plan complex; principal block, two storeys terminating in a round tower. Huge gable window facing east.

Templelands

ACKNOWLEDGEMENTS & BIBLIOGRAPHY

The authors are particularly indebted to the staff of West Lothian District Council, Conservation Unit, the Planning Department, and the Central Library; to Mr & Mrs W Cadell for continuous help, interest and hospitality; Thom Pollock, The Pollock Hammond Partnership; Sybil Cavanagh, Bathgate Central Library; George McNeil, George Paterson, Stuart Eydmann and Graham Reid at West Lothian District Council, for a wealth of help and material; The Appleton Partnership; Tom Duncan; Sir Anthony Wheeler; Gordon Davies and Jack Hugh at Livingston Development Corporation; Tom Robertson for invaluable information on.the history of Bathgate; Martin Lawrence; Alan Tuffs; Professor David Walker; Tam and Kathleen Dalyell; Rob Ridder; Martin Garden and John Cunningham at Lothian Regional Architects; Ian McCrorie; Bernadette Goslin; Hamish Haswell-Smith; Professor Brian Edwards; Mr & Mrs William Nimmo; Richard Ewing; The Bennie Museum; Margaret Wilson; Ian Gow, Jane Thomas and the staff of the National Monuments Record of Scotland; the Photographic Librarian, Historic Scotland; Simpson & Brown; William Nimmo & Partners. In particular, special thanks are due to Helen Leng, Wendy Gardiner, Dorothy Smith, Margaret Letham and to Avril Jaques for a keen pair of eyes, much patience and forbearance.

For permission to reproduce photographs, specific thanks are due to Historic Scotland; Angus and Patricia Macdonald; Mike Henderson of Dick Peddie & McKay; Forth Studios; John & Jean Fooks; The Parr Partnership; The Holmes Partnership; The National Trust for Scotland; RIAS Library; RIAS Drawings Collection; Stewart Tod & Partners; Lothian Regional Council; West Lothian District Council; Livingston Development Corporation; the Trustees of the Sir John Soane Museum; M D Allen; Lothian Studio; and the National Library of Scotland, for the Timothy Pont maps.

References
Linlithgow in Pictures, Angus MacDonald, A & C Black, 1932; **Landscape Illustrations of the Waverley Novels**, London, 1832; **Scotland Described (Edinburgh)**, 1806; **The Highlands - a 19th-century Tour**, J E Bowman, 1827; **Scotland Delineated (Edinburgh)**, 1799, R Heron; **Across the Tweed**, Theodor Fontane, 1858; **Early Travellers in Scotland**, P Hume Brown (Edinburgh), reprint 1973; **The Discovery of Scotland**, Maurice Lindsay, London, 1979; **The Eye is Delighted**, Maurice Lindsay, London, 1971; **Journal of Lord Cockburn**, Edinburgh, 1874; **Beauties of Scotland**, R W Forsyth, 1806; **Pennant's Tour in Scotland**, Thomas Pennant, London, 1772; **Tour Through the Whole Island of Great Britain**, Daniel Defoe (London reprint), 1983; **Linlithgow**, W F Hendrie, Edinburgh, 1989; **A History of the Town and Palace of Linlithgow**, George Waldie, 1858; **Medieval Religious Houses, Scotland**, Cowan & Easson, London, 1976; **Reginald Fairlie**, Patrick Nuttgens, Edinburgh, 1959; **Discovering West Lothian**, W F Hendrie, 1986; **Forth to the Sea**, W F Hendrie, 1980; **Topographical and Historical Account of Linlithgowshire**, J Penney; **History of St Michael's Church**, Dr John Ferguson; **West Lothian Place Names**, J G Wilkinson; **Sanctuary and the Privilege of St John**, P H R Mackay; **Sudden Slaughter: the Murder of the Regent Moray**, Patric Cadell, West Lothian History & Amenity Society; **Ordnance Gazetteer of Scotland**, Francis Groome, 1892; **First, Second** and **Third Statistical Accounts of Scotland**; **Lothian**, Buildings of Scotland series, Colin McWilliam, 1978; **A Lothian Village**, Martin Lawrence; **History of Mid Calder**, McCall, 1893; **Industrial Archaeology of Scotland**, John Hume, 1976; **Country Life in Scotland: Our Rural Past**, A Fenton, 1987; **The Bangour Story: A History of Bangour Village and General Hospitals**, W F Hendrie & D A D MacLeod, 1991; **Exploring Scotland's Heritage: Lothian & The Borders**, John R Baldwin (RCAHMS); **The Castellated and Domestic Architecture of Scotland**, David MacGibbon & Thomas Ross, 1897; **Understanding Scottish Graveyards**, Betty Wilsher, 1985; **The Story of the Forth**, Henry M Cadell; **The Rocks of West Lothian**, Henry M Cadell; **Buildings of the Scottish Countryside**, R J Naismith, 1985; **Forth & Clyde Canal Guide Book**, Paul Carter, 1985; **Bathgate Hills**, West Lothian District Council Leisure & Recreation Department; **Cairnpapple**, Stuart Piggott, 1985; **The Rural Architecture of Scotland**, Alexander Fenton & Bruce Walker.

1. Architrave (projecting ornamental frame)
2. Astragal (glazing bar)
3. Barge (gable board)
4. Basement, raised
5. Bullseye, keyblocked (circular window with projecting blocks punctuating frame)
6. Buttress (supporting projection)
7. Caphouse (top chamber)
8. Cartouche (decorative tablet)
9. Cherrycocking (masonry joints filled with small stones)
10. Channelled ashlar (recessed horizontal joints in smooth masonry)
11. Chimneycope, corniced
12. Chimneycope, moulded
13. Close (alley)
14. Cobbles
15. Console (scroll bracket)
16. Corbel (projection support)
17. Crowsteps
18. Cutwater (wedge-shaped end of bridge pier)
19. Doocot, lectern
20. Dormer, canted & piended
21. Dormer, pedimented (qv) wallhead
22. Dormer, piended (see under 'roof')
23. Dormer, swept wallhead
24. Fanlight (glazed panel above door)
25. Finial (crowning ornament)
26. Fly-over stair
27. Forestair, pillared
28. Gable, wallhead
29. Gable, wallhead chimney
30. Gable, Dutch (curved)
31. Gibbs doorway (framed with projecting stonework)
32. Harling
33. Hoist, fishing net
34. Hoodmoulding (projection over opening to divert rainwater)
35. Jettied (overhanging)
36. Lucarne (small dormer on spire)
37. Margin, stone
38. Mercat Cross
39. Marriage Lintel
40. Mullion (vertical division of window)
41. Nave (main body of church)
42. Pavilion (building attached by wing to main building)
43. Pediment (triangular ornamental feature above windows etc)
44. Portico
45. Quoins, rusticated (corner stones with recessed joints)
46. Refuge (recess in bridge parapet)
47. Ridge, crested
48. Roof, flared pyramidal
49. Roof, leanto
50. Roof, ogival (with S-curve pitch generally rising from square plan and meeting at point)
51. Roof, pantiled
52. Roof, piended (formed by intersecting roof slopes)
53. Roof, slated
54. Skew (gable coping)
55. Skewputt, moulded (lowest stone of skew, qv)
56. Skewputt, scroll
57. Stair jamb (projection containing stairway)
58. Stringcourse (horizontal projecting wall moulding)
59. Transept (transverse wing of cruciform church)
60. Transom (horizontal division of window)
61. Voussoir (wedge-shaped stone forming archway)
62. Tympanum (area within pediment qv)
63. Window, bay (projecting full-height from ground level)
64. Window, oriel (corbelled bay qv)
65. Window, sash & case (sliding sashes within case)

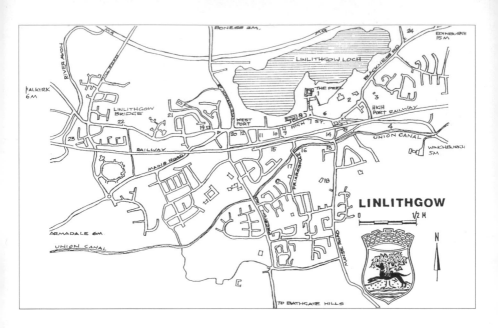

LINLITHGOW

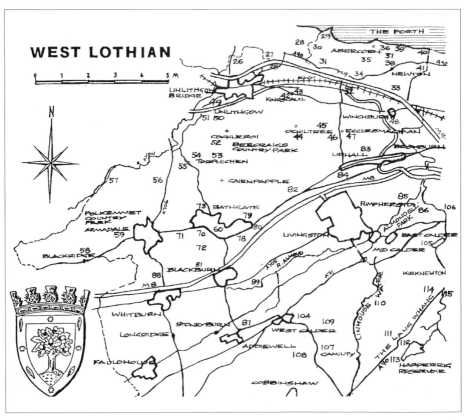

WEST LOTHIAN